KUDOS FROM THE BIG GUNS

"Suzanne (with Jean Ketcham) has always modeled the way vibrant women lead through collaboration and humor as they age. This book adds other signature gifts: practical advice and style. I love it!"

Stephen Reily, Founder & Chairman Vibrant Nation.com

"C. Suzanne Bates' essays are laugh-out-loud funny, but they're far more than that. They're chock-full of insight and introspection garnered over many years by a gracious and good-hearted survivor of life's inevitable challenges. There is no self-pity in these pages—just warmth and wisdom to inspire readers to bring fulfillment, happiness and some awesome Feng shui into their own lives."

Gail Rosenblum, columnist, Star Tribune, and author of *A Hundred Lives Since Then: Essays on Motherhood, Marriage, Mortality and More*

"Although I have yet to pee on a sofa or flung myself from an airplane with a parachute strapped to my back, I could entirely relate to this wonderfully entertaining book. I laughed…. actually roared hysterically, nodded my head in agreement and teared up at times while reading this. Suzanne captures the adventure of aging by showing all of us "mature" broads that although we might be growing older we don't have to necessarily grow up. It's fun, poignant and yes…..a dangerous stage of our life and this book shows us how to embrace these wonderful years."

Linda Fiterman, Author of *From Colic to College*, Philanthropist

"At 86 years old I skydived with Aging But DANGEROUS! I love these women! They are making a difference in the way women think about aging! Suzanne is a wonderful writer. I enjoyed the book so much! I hope for her many blessings."

Sister Rosalind Gefre, The Sisters of St Joseph of Carondelet

"C. Suzanne Bates, a truly Aging But DANGEROUS woman, has delivered in spades. There is much knowledge to be gleaned from this entertaining and humorous book. With her more than forty years of design experience, she creates an exciting and easy guide on how to beautifully and uniquely design your personal spaces. From advice on color and light to practical and simple steps, Suzanne gives high impact solutions to recharge your life and home. I can't say enough about her passion for great design—design that is lasting and timeless!"

Christine Frisk ASID, President Minnesota Chapter ASID, CEO InUnison Design, Co-Founder & President Fuse Studio

"I have known Suzanne and Jean for many years, and appreciate the work they are doing with Aging But DANGEROUS. As we all age we must deal with lots of changes and Suzanne and Jean are helping us to laugh at them rather than cry. It is a great contribution.

This book has lots of fun stories and helps us to not only laugh but it also gives some very helpful information about how to handle some of our new challenges. Thanks you, Suzanne. Great book. I highly recommend it."

Bobbie Stevens, Ph.D. Psychologist, Founder and CEO of Unlimited Futures LLC, Author – *UNLIMITED FUTURES – How To Understand the Life You Have & Creates the Life You Want*

"With love and honor I recommend *DON'T PEE ON MY SOFA!* It contains excellent advice, "butt" most importantly, Suzanne cracks me up. Her stories are funny, she is full of wit and wisdom and there is no one I respect and love more— she is my GURU."

Abra Coleman (too many certifications to list), Fitness Guru & Educator (Ann Landers' granddaughter)

"Suzanne and Jean have been friends of mine for many years. They're great role models for all of us experiencing this aging process. Having been in professional counseling and coaching for over 50 years myself, I know how powerful humor can be. Even though I am of the opposite sex, well over 50% of my clients through the years have been females. And that's the reason I appreciate the sometimes subtle, sometimes risqué, and many times just good common sense that brings out the humor and laughter in this book.

Suzanne has done an outstanding job in relating actual experiences which will bring a chuckle. And this humor and laughter again is one of the most powerful factors in helping all of us age gracefully. Thanks, Suzanne, for this delightful book and I know it'll have a wonderful healing effect on the reader."

Dean Portinga, Th.D. Ph.D., Founder & CEO, Spiritual Insights

"Anyone going through the many challenges of aging, even beginning in their 40's, will appreciate the candor and information filled essays in this book. Suzanne dispels many myths of aging one humorous essay at a time. A delightful and often poignant read!"

Chef Larry Fournillier, Founder, Larry Fourmillier Flavoring The World One Pot At A Time

"Filled with expert wisdom this extremely well written book has tapped into the hearts and souls of the 40+ year old woman. *DON'T PEE ON MY SOFA!*, will enrich and inspire you, (as it did me). Suzanne is adamant about the ability of all women to fly in the face of preconceived norms and tackle any obstacle that stands in the way of fulfilling their dreams. That philosophy, and how to get there, comes through loud and clear in this book."

Linda Walton Rouhani, Founder & CEO, Woodcliffe Speakers Bureau

DON'T PEE ON MY SOFA

AND OTHER THINGS TO LAUGH ABOUT

C. SUZANNE BATES
Co-Founder, AgingButDANGEROUS.com

Copyright 2015 C. Suzanne Bates

Cover Design by Michelle Fairbanks/Fresh Design

Edited by Hal Clifford

ISBN 978-0-9976157-0-8

EPUB ISBN 978-0-9976157-2-2

Library of Congress Control Number: 2015916504

For my Mom who at 90 years old can still be the most glamorous, funniest, wisest person in the room

Ruthie Bates at 90+ and Me

TABLE OF CONTENTS

PREFACE •• Why? **13**
MY PARTNER IN CRIME **15**
"DROPPING IN" WITH US **16**

YOU MAY NOT HAVE URINATED ON A DEAR FRIEND'S SOFA, BUT WE ALL HAVE STORIES! **19**
    DON'T PEE ON MY SOFA **20**
    THE EMERGENCY SQUAT: Not a Yoga Pose **23**

NOBODY EVER DIED FROM BAD DESIGN, BUT IT SURE CAN MAKE YOU FEEL CRUMMY **27**
    WHAT GOES UP MUST COME DOWN: A Material Purge **28**
    DOES SIZE REALLY MATTER? **32**
    FIT TO BE TRIED **34**
        FORENSIC DESIGN TIPS OVERVIEW **35**
        NEW DIGS 101 **37**
        A DIFFERENT ANGLE **41**
        A NEW PERSPECTIVE **45**
    ENVIRONMENT = ATTITUDE **48**
    FEELING SCRAPPY **52**
    FEELING COCKY? A Reason to Crow **55**
    MOVIN' ON **58**

A CLASSIC RE-BIRTH—JUST LIKE US **60**
WHAT YOU "SEE" IS WHAT YOU GET! **63**

DIRTY LITTLE SECRETS   **67**
GETTING TRASHED **68**
OFF THE WALL GARDENS **70**
THE GRASS IS ALWAYS GREENER... **72**

EXPOSE YOURSELF TO REALITY   **73**
PRIVATE OR PUBIC **74**
UPON REFLECTION **75**
WHEN YOU'RE HOT, YOU'RE HOT **76**
DEFINE SEXY **80**
OVER-EXPOSURE **83**
HAIR-RAISING! **86**
GOT BALLS? **88**
STAND UP STRAIGHT **90**
THE EYES HAVE IT! A Brow-Beating **92**
TOE TO TOE **95**
STARVING – OR DOES IT JUST LOOK THAT WAY? **97**

DON'T BE A TOTAL BOOB   **101**
HEAVY LIFTING? **102**
NOT A PERFECT PAIR **104**
KEEPING ABREAST **106**

IF LOOKS COULD KILL   **111**
"DON'T DRINK AND DRESS" **112**
SKIRTING THE ISSUE **114**
JEAN'S JEANS **116**
BOOGIE ON DOWN: A Casting Call **119**
MODEL BEHAVIOR **122**

JAZZED UP AND GORGEOUS! **124**
DOES HE NEED A SPANXING? **128**
RUTHIE'S SHOE REJUVENATION **131**

BLINDED BY THE LIGHT **135**
A FRENCH CONNECTION **136**
IN YOUR ZONE **140**
I'VE SEEN THE LIGHT **143**

TELL ME, WHAT IS IT YOU PLAN TO DO WITH YOUR ONE WILD AND PRECIOUS LIFE? **146**
DECIDE TO LIVE **148**
REACH! **151**

RESOURCES **153**
PHOTO CREDITS **157**
THANKS, MOM…! **162**
ABOUT THE AUTHOR **163**
MORE GREAT READS FROM BOOKTROPE **167**

The question isn't who is going to let me;
it's who is going to stop me.

•••Ayn Rand

PREFACE ·· Why?

MY WEDDING VOWS should have given me more insight into what would lie ahead in my life: "Richer, poorer, sickness and health..." ups and downs, smitten hearts, broken hearts, heart attacks, big breasts, sagging breasts, and, for some of my friends, no breasts. Being ever more perplexed about how I look with each passing year. (Has the expression "she's hot" disappeared from my life forever?) And sex... even bringing up the word paralyzes me: where? how? when? and with whom (or what)?

The heartfelt essays on the following pages are about all of us sage women—that includes you—and how we are surviving and thriving in these, the teeter-totter years of our lives.

For the past six years, AgingButDANGEROUS.com has given Jean Ketcham and me the opportunity to empower, inspire, inform, and challenge women who were baffled about "what's next." From this platform, we have seen women reduce their "buts" (one "t", not two) and recapture dreams they had forgotten they'd even had. We applaud them, support them, and share their joy through these stories.

Wellness, money, matters of the heart, sex, how we look, our ever-evolving and descending mammaries, "dangerous" tales and practical tips that go beyond our preconceived notions about what we can or should be—we address all of this lovingly and humorously. Really, how else can we?

Grab a cup of tea or a well-deserved martini. Learn, laugh, and leisurely absorb the knowledge and inspiration within these pages. Among these numerous jewels you may also find the courage to say to your most cherished friend, "Please, Don't Pee On My Sofa."

MY PARTNER IN CRIME

FOR MORE THAN thirty-five years, my life has been enriched by Jean Ketcham, first as a much-needed friend and eventually as a business partner. To say I love her falls far short of the depth of emotion I have for her. Without her, I never would have accomplished this book. Her input may be undetectable to the reader, but she has edited, critiqued, poo-pooed, amended, and cheer-led all of the work in front of you.

Thank you, Jeanie, for the multitude of blessings you bring to my entire life. You are greatly cherished!

"DROPPING IN" WITH US

__Woman, 90, skydives to prove age is just a number__ (Feb., 2, 2002): Mami Evans literally "dropped in" for her 90th birthday party Saturday afternoon, jumping from an airplane cruising over her farm at 12,000 feet.

She said she wanted to show her friends that age is just a state of mind, even when you're nearing the century mark.

WE LOVE MAMI—she is what being Aging But DANGEROUS is all about.

Although Da Vinci sketched the design for the first parachute in 1485 (which, by the way, still works), it took Jean Ketcham another 500-plus years to try the slightly updated version available today. She loved it!

Somehow this breathtaking thrill has become a rite of passage, a symbol of undying youth. Whether you're the first former President Bush or Jean's dad, who jumped at 91, if you want to show the world that life can be exciting at any age—*JUMP*!

When Jean jumped in 2000 at sixty years of age, with her dad, she muttered a reluctant, "No... no," as she and her tandem buddy instructor neared the open door of the airplane. He told her he thought she said, "Go, go!" (yeah, right), and so began her exhilarating 14,000-foot drop. She fell 174 feet per fabulous second and loved the invigorating rush. Could we say it was airgasmic?

Then, in August of 2010, Jean informed friends and members of our Aging But DANGEROUS online community of her upcoming plans to celebrate her seventieth birthday with a second jump. Once again, she planned to rise to the heavens and then rapidly descend via a parachute. She had a surprising response. *"We want to do it, too,"* actually came out of their mouths. Not mine!

There would be a ton of fun activities for those of us firmly planted on terra firma, and special Aging But DANGEROUS martinis would be served to our brave participants when they once again attached themselves to planet earth. That reward would almost be worth me jumping out of an airplane. (We felt the "medical martini" might quell the anxiety of a friend or family member on the ground as they saw their loved ones falling toward them from thousands of feet in the air, so we decided to make the martinis available for all.) A giant screen would then broadcast a review of their in-flight video, so all of us on the ground would be able share their ecstasy (or their terror). Feelings of reassured courage and strengthened self-worth would certainly run rampant throughout the entire drop zone.

How many women would show up and actually participate? We had no idea. What we did know was that we had made the opportunity available to all who had long been harboring a desire to skydive, as well as those who were contemplating it for the first time.

Oh, and Jean's dad wants to jump with her again, at the age of 101 (but his ninety-eight-year-old *new* wife won't let him; she is such a buzz kill).

There are ongoing choices in our lives about facing our fears or pursuing our dreams that can change our lives forever. The stories on the following pages may help you decide whether or not you are going to join Jean on her next skydive? It's all up to you!

YOU MAY NOT HAVE URINATED ON A DEAR FRIEND'S SOFA...

BUT WE ALL HAVE STORIES!

DON'T PEE ON MY SOFA

WHEN MY KIDS were growing up, I decided they needed a grandmother figure in their lives. Our own parents were either deceased or geographically unavailable, so we "adopted" an older woman from our church as a surrogate grandmother. My vision was that this sweet older lady would bake cookies with my kids and speak dreamily to them about her childhood, as they hung spellbound on her every word.

Our reality was that this old coot turned out to be one of the meanest people I had ever known! Not only did she freak our kids out with her Billy Goat Gruff chin hairs; her final endearing gesture was urinating on the leather seats of my husband's new Jaguar. How could anyone pee in a new Jag? My husband (now my ex) refused to embrace her after that. I was not sad.

Several years later, while visiting some wonderful friends on their boat, I demonstrated a bizarre cheer about an obscure football team in the Big Ten. Instead of focusing on my bouncy little cheer, though, my friends began discussing uncontrollable urination. Why were these wonderfully chic women saying things like, "Yeah, wait until you're our age, and you won't be bouncing up and down like that anymore. You'll be wetting your pants if you do"? *REALLY?* I was totally perplexed.

Recently, my partner Jean, her husband Mike, and I were having dinner with some very close, longtime friends. At some point during the evening, Jean announced, "I'm wetting my pants every time I laugh." *REALLY?* I thought.

After dinner, we moved to the living room, and the true dilemma of her situation became a virtual sitcom clip. Jean suggested that she sit on a nearby pillow, so as not to wet the furniture. The host announced, "I don't want you peeing on our pillow!" Our hostess suggested she sit on the leather couch. Jean was just trying to be a responsible guest and said that she was uncomfortable wetting their leather sofa! Finally, a towel appeared, and the mini-crisis was averted in a manner that suited all involved parties.

These situations may have been a surprise to me, but they shouldn't have been. In the United States, thirteen million adults suffer from urinary incontinence (UI). According to *What Your Female Patients Want To Know About Bladder Control*, one in four women between the ages of thirty and fifty-nine deal with UI. According to the Agency for Health Care Policy and Research (AHCPR), Americans spend $11.2 billion yearly on pads and adult diapers to manage UI. That figure will be rising as we boomers progress in age.

There are numerous other websites to answer your questions, give you support, and share the latest data concerning this challenge. If you want to know more about this all-too-common problem, check out the links in my Resources section at the back of this book!

Thank you, wonderful friend and business partner Jean, for bringing to the forefront a subject that, although not terribly appealing, is one that I am afraid is going to be with us for many years to come. I hope you are not offended by the towel, monogrammed with your initials and permanently secured to the shotgun seat of my car. Think of it as a tribute to your integrity. Yeah, that's it.

A Brief Diversion: How to Remove Urine Stains from Upholstery

- Blot the urine stain using a cloth.
- Mix one tablespoon of dishwashing liquid with two cups of cold water in a small bowl.
- Dip a clean white cloth into the solution.
- Using a dry cloth (with no solution), gently blot the affected area until it's dry. Repeat three more times.

THE EMERGENCY SQUAT
Not a Yoga Pose

PUBLIC URINATION IS clearly a "no-no." But what happens when the choice is either to wet your pants or drop your drawers? For those of you feeling ashamed of those leakage issues—*don't*. Many of us are arriving upon the threshold of the perpetually moist crotch. It's just where we are in the aging process.

While driving from Minnesota a couple of years ago, I began to feel the urge to urinate. Pretty common bodily function; very ordinary sensation; nothing unusual. By the time I found an exit with any signs of life, I was in full emergency mode and instructing myself out loud in a stern, authoritarian voice. I was panicked, holding my crotch like I was five years old and driving with my free hand. *Where was the gas station the highway sign had promised?* Nowhere in sight!

I took a desperate turn down a city street. A vacant lot presented itself just to my left. It had moderate privacy from the busy street. Driving my VW Beetle right onto the lot, I crouched behind the open door for privacy and did the unthinkable. I bared my back side, squatted, and let her go. *Ahhh,* relief—and just in the nick of time!

Amazingly, I felt nothing but relief: no guilt, no shame, no embarrassment—just contentment. Listen, girl-friends, let's not get all huffy and judgmental about this. When you gotta go—you gotta go! One in three "older people" have some form of incontinence, although it is most common in women. Our Aging But DANGEROUS prediction is that we are going to see a lot more of this peculiar behavior as more of us hit sixty.

My self-diagnosis is that I am experiencing the beginning stages of the most common type of a pesky predicament called "urge incontinence." Urge incontinence is when you have an abrupt and intense urge to urinate, followed by an uncontrollable loss of urine. No clear cause can be identified for this condition, but lack of estrogen (menopause), full bowels (constipation), and obesity can contribute negatively.

There is medication; your doctor can recommend the best one for your situation. Also, lifestyle modifications can help manage and even cure this potentially embarrassing condition. Follow the Mayo Clinic link in our Resources section below and take responsibility for your own health.

For me, it's a new regime of Kegels (repetitive contractions of the pelvic muscles that control the flow in urination in order to strengthen these muscles, especially to control or prevent incontinence or to enhance sexual responsiveness during intercourse). Or some simulated form of vaginal contractions. Like a sex toy. Who ever thought my vagina would need to do push-ups?

Also, drink lots of water, although that seems counterintuitive. Drinking too little fluid can lead to increased amounts of body-waste products in your urine. Highly concentrated urine is dark yellow and has a strong smell. It can irritate your bladder, increasing the urge and frequency with which you need to go.

This was helpful information for me, from www.EverydayHealth.com:

> "Many people who have urinary incontinence think they should drink less water to decrease the risk of an accident. But this isn't exactly true. While drinking too much fluid can lead to bladder leakage, not drinking enough can also lead to leakage and bladder health problems. 'When you don't drink enough water, the urine becomes more concentrated and that can be irritating to the bladder and increase urgency,' says Tomas Griebling, MD, MPH, vice-chair of the department

of urology at the University of Kansas Medical Center in Kansas City. So it's important to keep a healthy balance of fluids.

"Certain medications, such as diuretics, some blood pressure medications, and antidepressants, can cause urinary incontinence, so talk to your doctor about any prescription and over-the-counter drugs you are taking. 'Bring as many of your medications as possible with you to the doctor,' says Griebling. With more information, your doctor can better identify your type of urinary incontinence and what factors might be affecting you, which is important for treatment"

They also have a Managing Urinary Incontinence Guide on their website.

I rely on Solaray CranActin chewables, which I have taken since a urinary tract infection almost did me in several years ago—they seem to help. At the first sign of bladder pressure, I find a toilet, I carry extra tissues and I practice my squats religiously in exercise class—just in case.

NOBODY EVER DIED FROM BAD DESIGN

But it sure can make you feel crummy

WHAT GOES UP MUST COME DOWN
A Material Purge

 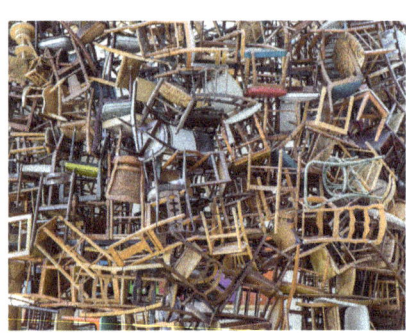

DOWNSIZING SEEMS TO be a reality of our times. The relocation epidemic is upon us, encompassing everyone from survivors of Bernie Madoff's perfidy to people who just want to live in warmer climates and actually feel their extremities after winter arrives. In too many cases, though, relocating is a product of unpredicted, unwelcome change: loss of a spouse, dwindling finances, employment issues—all can be triggers. Inevitable personal growth *will* accompany such a transition, like it or not.

Recently I heard about a woman who had just been forced to part with eight of her ten sofas. Her new digs could only accommodate two sofas—bummer! Getting too teary-eyed over that predicament might seem to be a stretch—unless you know the sad backstory of lost health and suffering that contributed to the debacle. Very few of us are immune from these often unpredictable periods of readjustment and conciliation.

Yet shrinking one's living space can also be a joyous journey riddled with opportunities. Let's hope this is your scenario. Distillation usually adds much flavor and richness to any circumstance—think of this as your opportunity to create a tasty reduction of possessions. Ludwig Mies Van Der Rohe, one of the founders of modern architecture, is associated with the term "less is more"—and he was born in 1866. This concept is *not new*.

In 2009, I packed twenty years of my life, previously housed in 6,000 square feet of my home, and moved into a space that, optimistically speaking, **may** have been slightly over 700 square feet. Then, in 2014, I returned to Minneapolis to an even smaller apartment. This topic is fresh and very real to me. Here are some of the things that helped my transition. (It's like childbirth: if you could remember what it felt like, you would never do it again. After that first experience, the thought of ever moving again gave me a contraction.)

- Sort your belongings in small steps, if possible. This exercise is physically and emotionally draining. Every couple of hours, take a break and do something nice for yourself. (I played Motown and "danced as

if no one was watching"—because they weren't. *The Tina Turner in me rocks*.)
- Set up a system that works for you to identify what you keep, what you meaningfully gift to those for whom you care, what you sell, what you donate, what you store, what you give to people you have never liked (usually coming from the toss pile), and what you want/need to dispose of. Different colored stickers worked for me; some prefer lists or, when possible, physically moving items to areas designated to the above categories.
- Live with your choices for a while to make sure that they feel right. Do not change *anything* from pile to pile without intense scrutiny of your motivations. (After more than one glass of wine, *do not go near those piles*.)

Be sure to ask your kids and other interlopers to remove their stuff from your personal space (in a sweet way of course—my kids were my worst offenders).

If you begin in small rooms where few decisions are necessary, by the time you get to the daunting stuff, you will be more experienced, and the mental calluses combined with how sick you are of this entire exercise will work to your advantage. Call your buddies in for support—good friends usually make wonderful counsel when you're vacillating about anything.

Start now, no matter what your situation—sooner or later you will be dealing with the recirculation of material possessions. And it feels oh-so-good to cleanse. Mies clearly knew how truly wonderful it feels to purge.

Find some great additional online information in the Resources section.

> ### A Brief Diversion: REDUCE YOUR "BUT"!
>
> It seems like BIG BUTS are soooo prevalent—in my conversations, that is, and clearly in people's lives.
>
> - "I would like to sort through all my stuff—BUT."
> - "I would like to ride my bike more—BUT."
> - "I would like to paint my dining room red—BUT."
>
> What's with all of the excuses, women? Make it happen! If there is something that you want to do—expend the effort to find out *HOW* to make it possible. If you will invest some energy to live your dreams—and that's obviously much more fun than de-cluttering your home—your life will be glorious, and immense joy will prevail.
>
> Smaller "buts" make for fuller, happier lives.
>
> How big is your "but"?

DOES SIZE REALLY MATTER?

KANSAS CITY WAS a great place to lick my wounds and heal from the painful loss of most of my material possessions through bankruptcy, the loss of my spouse, and the loss of a lifestyle that few could ever imagine. Having grown up in Missouri, I returned there to be close to family, old friends, and traditions that were familiar and comforting.

In 2014, I had garnered enough strength to head back to Minneapolis. It had become clear during my nearly six-year sabbatical that Minneapolis was my home, and it was where I truly wanted to be. The big problem lurking beneath the obvious euphoria of my return was the substantial increase in the cost of living in the North Country. The places where I felt comfortable living far exceeded my budget.

Apartments that fell within my cost allowance were miniscule in size. *Could I really do this shrinking act again?* Like most situations in life, when I am put to the task, I amaze myself as to what I am capable of doing. My new apartment, in the precise area I loved and had envisioned living, was a whopping 351 square feet in size. Smaller than my closet from eight years prior. In these new digs, I was able to fit an entry space (complete with chair), TV "room"/library, "great" room, dining area, kitchen, sleeping area that I like to call the master suite, and office.

In the following notes I will share my most recent journey, some tricks of the trade, and some systematic approaches that will give you hope and inspiration for your next relocation. Dare I say I feel it's quite moving? (Or, you'll feel a moving connection...!)

FIT TO BE TRIED

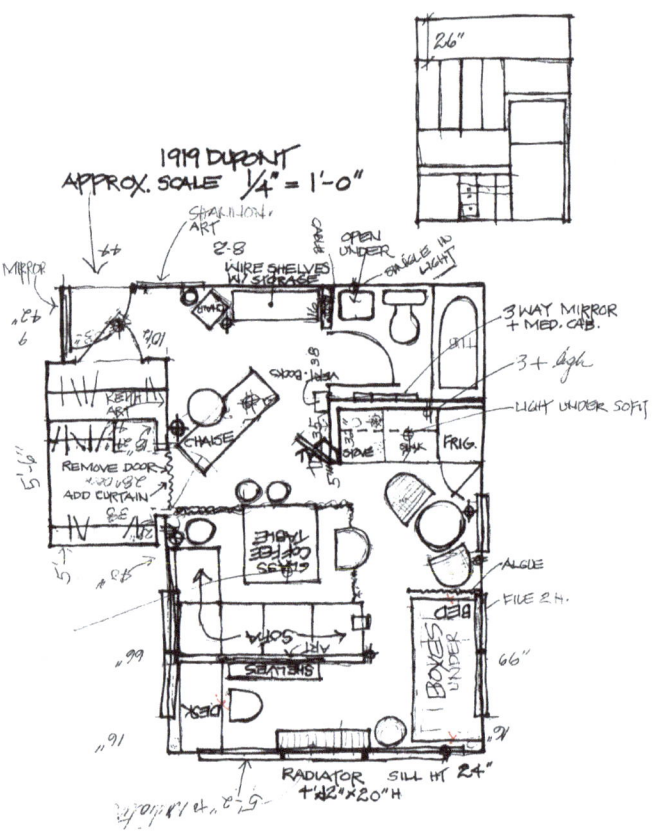

AFTER OVER FORTY YEARS as a certified and credentialed interior designer, and at one time as owner of one of the largest interior design firms in Minneapolis, I gleaned much practical knowledge. The following design piece I share with you in the hope that it will lessen your stress and help make your transition smoother and more joyous.

FORENSIC DESIGN TIPS OVERVIEW

- Choose a place with as many windows as possible. Light really opens up a small space, as well as your heart.
- My all-white bathroom with a window gives me the choice to go any color direction and also to flash the neighbors when I'm showering. (If anyone wants to look at this sixty-seven-year-old body, who am I to stop them?)
  - Using clear shower curtains both to cover the large window and also as the primary shower curtain opens up light and space. Having no visual barriers increases the feeling of size.
  - Adding a thin-profile, surface-mounted medicine cabinet with three mirrored doors (to create a three-way mirror) is a must for me. Additional storage and mandatory hair interventions are made easy with this inexpensive accessory, making this a "must have" tool. (It doesn't even have to be in the bathroom, if there is not enough wall space. This piece can be utilized in many areas.)
- Incandescent lighting adds warmth, softness, and forgiveness to wrinkles on all parts of the body.
- Fluorescent lighting in most cases is harsh, unflattering, and of a light quality that you don't want to live with by choice. That's why God made floor lamps.
- *ALWAYS* measure your new space yourself to confirm any dimensions given you by a landlord, leasing agent, or former now-displaced boyfriend. Do the same with your furniture. Use 1/4" gridded paper to make a scale map of the rooms and see if, and how, your existing furniture fits.

- 1/4" = 1'. Think one full square is 12"; for 6", you use half a square and so on.
- Radiators can be great shelves if the material you put on top of them conducts minimal heat. (I learned about some options here: http://www.apartmenttherapy.com/-good-questions-16-29316.) This detail was much trickier than I anticipated. The existing glass shelf I used was not ideal. Hooks are great for small spaces and many, many purposes. No plastic hooks in visible spaces—nice hooks only.
- Mirrors located at the ends of hallways and where light can be reflected are always welcome. Ikea is a great source for mirrors.
- Area rugs that blend with the floor color can help create zones. In small spaces, you don't want your area rug to clutter the space visually. Area rugs over carpet can also work beautifully, not just esthetically but to act as a barrier between you and the scuzz the former occupants may have left behind (even if the rugs were cleaned prior to occupancy).
- Higher ceilings give you more options to expand vertically. The difference between 8' and 9' ceilings is *HUGE*. Don't guess; measure.
- Minimal window coverings that blend with the wall and window frames occupy less space both physically and visually.
- Light, neutral wall colors work best for small spaces in most cases. Bathrooms/powder rooms are great places to use strong color. If you are using the bathroom as a place to apply makeup, remember: bright colors will reflect off a mirror onto your skin, and ultra-dark colors

will eat your light, decreasing visibility in reflecting mirrors. I call that the Triple Martini Effect.
- Many times, replacing an interior door with a curtain can save you an immense amount of basically wasted floor space while softening an interior. Door swings can be evil culprits that stand in the way of you using more of your treasured furnishings. Coming out of the closet is also much more dramatic.

PHOTO TAKEN IN MY 14' X 14' APARTMENT TOWARD WEST-FACING WINDOWS
(All furnishings and accessories were existing.)

NEW DIGS 101

- Furnishings that blend with the walls have the effect of expanding the feel of the apartment. Neutral furnishings don't lock you into colors or patterns that might become outdated.

- The natural hemp rug from Ikea ($99) is soft to walk on and soft on the eyes. It defines a space with texture, not color.
- A large piece of art hangs as a separation between the "great room" and the office area. The files, printer, reference books, and utilitarian office mess is hidden by a visually pleasing element. Suspending art from the ceiling is not something I would ever do unless absolutely necessary. My art-collector friends probably are appalled.
- The shelf hovering above the west bank of windows solved the problem of my many and beloved books and equestrian trophies. If possible, run shelving wall to wall to create an architectural element as opposed to a decorative element. (I also used a vertical bookshelf beside the wall-mounted TV.)
- A real bummer was that I couldn't fit both a standard bed and an office in the space. I settled for a twin. Not a very positive statement about my love life, is it? When I get in bed at night, I keep waiting for my mom to show up to listen to my prayers.
- The clear Louis "Ghost" chair designed by architect/designer Philippe Starck in 2002 for Kartell. It provides utilitarian seating while occupying almost no visual space.
- A small (8" x 10") single-based tube table, in a great green accent color, moves easily to accommodate many tasks and positions in my small space.
- Two circular Kartell storage units, originally purchased from Max Beylerian, serve as bedside tables and provide tons of storage. They have been

repainted white, as the original white plastic had begun to yellow.
- An Algue modular wall hanging by Vitra is specifically shaped to provide a transparent, organic, and non-invasive separation between the sleeping area and the dining area. It can be reshaped to any size.
- White bedclothes allow the eye to flow seamlessly between the "great room" sofa sectional and the bed in the "master suite."
- The existing coffee table is large (40" x 40") but worked visually due to its transparency.
- White cotton-lend slipcovers were made for an existing sectional to cover a somewhat nauseating original fabric. They can easily be cleaned/washed. White blankets from Ikea can cover either the portion where I sit nightly or the entirety of the sofa for even more protection from grandchildren or my parents. (At the time of this book writing, my parents were ninety and a hundred, and occasionally, food unexpectedly escaped their mouths, just as it did my grandkids'.)
- The black fur ball pillow doubles as both a pet and an armrest.
- The TV is wall-mounted on a double-hinged swivel arm and can be seen from anyplace in the apartment. (Its reflection in the artwork enables me to follow shows even on a bathroom break. I know: TMI.)
- A mixture of floor lamps, table lamps, and under-counter lighting offer numerous options for light levels and atmosphere.
- The bed has been raised (all by me) to accommodate a two-high stack of cardboard file boxes (22" from

the bottom of the bed frame to the floor). This system (almost) replaced two five-drawer lateral filing cabinets. (*See diagram*.)
- Two of the Eames wooden stools float between living beneath the TV, when not in use, and deployment on the east side of the coffee table for additional seating. (The third stool in the Eames series lives in my closet.) I can simultaneously seat eleven friends cozily but comfortably for social events.
- Low-profile letter trays slide under the sofa to contain messy necessities (lip gloss, reading glasses, tissues, pens and paper, etc.) and a reading/computer tray.
- Reading glasses are at every possible location so they are convenient at all times. Without giving it too much thought, I just counted seven pairs in a 14' x 14' space. The eyes definitely have it!

PHOTO TAKEN IN MY 14' X 14' APARTMENT TOWARD EAST-FACING KITCHEN'

A DIFFERENT ANGLE

- 22"-diameter, round, yellow dining table folds and hangs on the wall if dancing should occur.
- The classic Bertoia side chair, designed by Harry Bertoia for Knoll (who still makes the chair), is another small, visually-lightweight chair that blends with any furniture style, especially antiques. This iconic wire furniture collection, introduced in 1952, is recognized worldwide as one of the great achievements of twentieth-century furniture design. My only complaint about these chairs, which I have owned for over twenty years and used in many diverse situations, is that if you sit on them naked, they leave big grid marks on your bum and thighs. This condition is not only unsightly but also painful.
- Algue by Vitra hangs at the end of the bed to subtly divide the sleeping area from the eating space. It's amazing how well something so transparent works to define a space.
- My horse trophies repeat a very subtle, low-key equestrian theme and reflect a little of who I am without speaking a word. The restrained use of my spurs and whips also seem to add interest, conversation points, and opportunities for humorous banter by male visitors. (They especially like the spurs.)
- The two rows of shelves above my kitchen nook house many necessary kitchen implements. Various-sized containers act as drawers.
- Lights added beneath the overhead kitchen cabinets to illuminate the countertops with clean bright light

provide a major benefit in this dingy area of the space. They look fantastic! Ikea has under-counter lighting for pennies, and it is one of the huge keys to creating a positive, pleasurable, environment.
- Black cords are wrapped with white duct tape. I taped all the cords together with the same white tape to organize them and make them visually disappear. This gives the appearance of spaciousness and/or someone who is mentally unbalanced.
- I painted the upper cabinets with charcoal-colored chalk board paint. Not only does the color blocking add interest to this area, it is very utilitarian and serves as a creative outlet, especially when I've been over-served.
- The Eames Walnut Stool (1960) originally was designed for the lobby and executive suites of the Time-Life Building at Rockefeller Center in New York City. I used these stools, 13.5" in diameter and 15" in height, for extra seating. They expand my seating capacity to eleven plus the edge of the bed. (Seating numbers vary depending on butt sizes.)
- The vertical bookshelf beside the TV houses fifty linear inches of books, plus another opportunity for a bronze horse trophy. (Think sculpture.) Google "vertical bookshelves" and you will find several different styles, manufacturers, and price points. (See detail photo)
- The extraordinarily small 292 Hill House 1 Ladderback dining chair designed by Charles Rennie Mackintosh in the early 1900s is a jewel for small spaces. (It is in the background to the left of

the white bin storage shelves.) Although its width is only 16.1" and its depth is a mere 13.8", because of it impressive height, 55.5", it holds its own with other standard-size furniture. It is a perfect piece to sit by the entry for dealing with removal of socks, boots, and shoes. Cassina is a resource for this chair and his entire oddly spectacular chair line.

- The Missoni towel I used in the kitchen area to pull all the color together was not easy to come by. Years ago I had to go to Milan, Italy to buy Missoni for my clients and myself. And I wasn't just telling my husband that to get an uncontested pass to Italy. I don't know what the situation is today. There isn't a better example of utility combined with good design and money spent effectively for getting maximum bang for your buck. Their website (http://www.missoni.com/us/missoni-home/themes_gid27528?menuseason=main) will give you what I think is only a part of the collection. (See detail photo)
- I recommend storing your toaster off the countertop on a shelf unless you think that's a crummy idea. In small spaces, keep countertops as empty and clean as possible to minimize the sense of clutter.
- See the white duct tape I used to wrap black cords? Not so much, right? It works! Use white cords if possible. They really cut the visual confusion in my "gourmet" kitchen.
- Although I used the top of the fridge for basket and vase storage, I still know what is in the cabinets behind my carefully curated collection. (See detail drawing below). I don't even need to open the

cabinet to know exactly what is in it. I keep this diagram on the inside of my lower kitchen cabinets. Diagramming works great for high shelves, too.

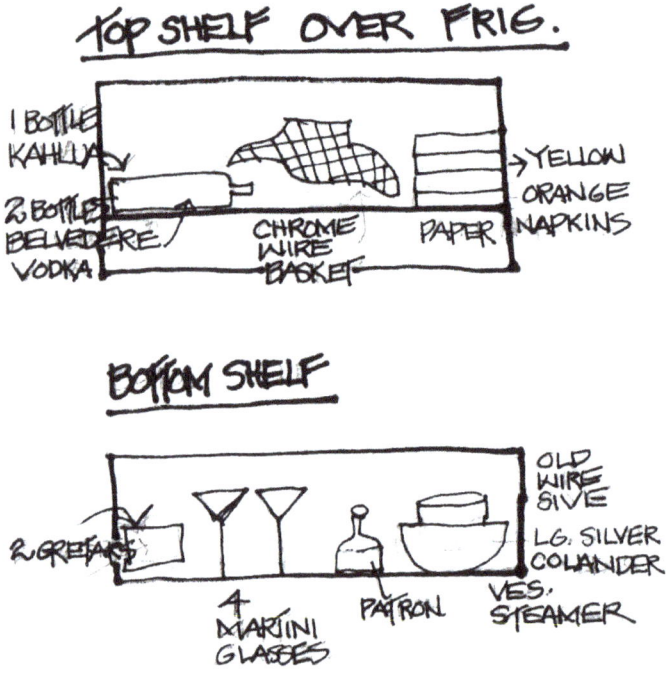

The following links will give you information on some of the pieces mentioned above:

https://www.google.com/#q=charles+rennie+mackintosh+furniture

http://www.yliving.com/category/Bath-Towels/Beach-Towels/_/N-3ku3kZ3ku34

PHOTO TAKEN IN MY 14' X 14' APARTMENT TOWARD NORTHEAST CORNER

A NEW PERSPECTIVE

- The closet door was removed to recapture valuable floor space. I added fabric to soften the area and provide a visual block into the closet.
- Ikea storage boxes constructed out of a tent-like fabric act as drawers for:
  - Linens and towels
  - Shoes, socks, and tights
  - Medicines and vitamins
  - Hair paraphernalia
  - Food
  - Junk (no matter how hard we try, we all have some)
- Wall mounting the TV saves floor space and adds flexibility.

- A nice-looking bag from The Walker Art Center serves as my recycling container. It also leads people to the false assumption that I can actually afford to shop there.
- My Le Corbusier Chaise Lounge is actually a little large for the space, but I felt it was worth making things a tad tight to be able to look at it daily. I enjoy its comfort when watching TV in the "TV room". This IS a give-and-take process.
- Hanging my large pieces of art in such a small wall space is not kosher; I do know better. I broke a lot of "rules" to achieve my desired end.
- Circular tables at the ends of a sofa and by chairs are easier to maneuver around than their square counterparts.

A Brief Diversion

- Lighten walls with SW6385 Dover White Sherwin Williams (800-474-3794; sherwin-williams.com. Or another favorite from the multitude of beautiful Benjamin Moore whites.
- Remove old carpeting and paint a strip "runner" or just an artsy accent stripe on stairs for only $20 in materials. Applying painter's tape guarantees crisp lines—or not.
- SUPER SPRAY PAINT—A single coat of Rust-Oleum Universal Spray paint covers any indoor or outdoor furniture or accessory. It's paint and primer in one for $6.78 (877-385-8155; rustoleum.com)
- DRY-ERASE TOPCOAT—New Sketch Pad clear-gloss finish turns a wall into a writing surface as easy to

clean as a dorm-room whiteboard. $49.99 for a kit from Sherwin-Williams (800-474.3794; sherwin-williams.com)

- CABINETRY COVERAGE—We can vouch for Waterborne Satin Impervo from Benjamin Moore. Kitchen cabinets will still look freshly painted in ten-plus years. $72.99 per gallon (885-724-6802; benjaminmoore.com)

ENVIRONMENT = ATTITUDE

FROM FLOCKED WALLPAPER to adhesive-backed mirror tiles (the smoked ones) to avocado appliances (boy, was that a mistake!), the environment in which we function has a huge impact on the way we feel. After over 35 years as a credentialed interior designer, I have embedded this fact deeply in my belief system. Fortunately, there are wonderful resources out there that will allow you to breathe new life into your surroundings on the cheap: Target, Ikea, Pier One, and sometimes even Wal-Mart.

Start by punching up just one room that no longer spins your wheels.

Add one new color to what has become a stale and boring space. The room will tell you what that color should be (unless your room is completely neutral, and then you can choose anything, as long as it knocks your socks off). Look around the room—look for a color that jazzes you up, that melts you! Maybe it's on an art object, in a pillow fabric, on dishes in a dining room, in a painting, maybe an area rug. Then listen closely as it whispers, "Choose me, choose me." If this sounds crazy to you, ask one of your more artsy friends—they can hear the voices. (Certainly you've figured that out by now.)

I am going to pick orange for my room. (If you live in a hot part of the country, then choose a cooler color or a very grayed-down orange.) So, why orange?

Here's why:

- It makes me feel happy inside!
- Orange has been a hot fashion color recently and products should be easy to find.
- There is a small amount of orange in both pieces of art in the room.
- Orange has loads of "kick."
- A small amount of orange exists in the sofa fabric, which is primarily red. (Your new color should relate to something already present.)

Decide on three or four new accessory pieces that can be spread around the room (usually not just in one chunk). In my case, I would add:

- A couple of orange pillows to the sectional.
- An orange throw to the ottomans at the foot of the bed. (Ikea has a great one, or did have at one point.)
- An orange bowl to the tiny modular kitchenette area.
- A small orange vase to the bedside table.

Periodically, I will test accent colors by using a piece of clothing or an object that I already own (like a sweater), just to make sure that I am on the right track.

Sure, you could get obsessive here and go into all the options and choices that will exist in any endeavor of this type. That is when people throw up their hands and walk away—when a project gets too complex and complicated. Small amounts of a vibrant color can bring your surroundings to life. Stick with a simple list and "just do it." You can do the above spiffing for around $100 (or possibly less) and some legwork. That's a lot of bang for your buck. If you don't have $100, just pop for a can of orange spray paint and look around for a few inanimate victims. Then head for the fabric store to acquire a little weekend pillow project. Where there is a will… you can kick butt—or something like that.

A Brief Diversion

- Feng Shui calls the color orange the "social" color, as it creates the feng shui energy to promote lively conversations and good times in your home—especially in the winter. We suggest you visit one of the many Feng Shui websites, like http://fengshui.about.com/od/fengshuicures/qt/fengshuicolor.htm. You wouldn't want to be sending some unknown crazy-ass signal to the universe.

- If you're not feeling well, try chromotherapy. Colors are specific wavelengths of electromagnetic energy seen through our eyes and can affect our feelings, moods, emotions, and maybe more. Wellness supposedly occurs when your colors are in balance.

- There are seven chakras in our bodies. In Ayurvedic medicine, each one has an associated color, organ, and function. Orange corresponds to the second chakra representing the functions of emotion and sexuality. Maybe we should take it easy on the orange.

- Go to the *Better Homes and Garden* Color-a-Room website to play in the virtual world before you make a big color commitment; it could save your sanity and your marriage. http://www.bhg.com/decorating/color/colors/welcome-to-color-a-room

FEELING SCRAPPY

AT THE RISK of being lynched by the scrapbooking mobs that roam this entire country, I don't get it. Disguised as sweet little parties, open-armed associations, stores with a sensitive heart, or just the bonding glue that adheres women's emotions to a sheet of acid free archival paper, scrapbooking and all its accoutrements are the rage.

We do need to preserve our fondest memories, that's obvious. Photos are some of life's most precious spoils. So why not the big-box approach? Or, if you have had no life or perhaps sport only minimal memories, the oversized shoe box will do, won't it?

First of all, I could live without a descriptive word that evoked visions so sweetie, sugary, sappy that I feel the need to purge after each utterance of the word… "scrapbooking." "Archiving" works best for me; it's much less gooey. Archiving sounds cleaner, crisper, more my style. Sorry, "scrappers!"

Now that I have addressed my own emotional inadequacies, I do remember finding a wonderful photo of me, taken when I first started showing horses over forty years ago, ruined by moisture damage. Had it been archived, I would still have that emotional trigger in order to relive that beautiful, stimulating time of my life.

Recording and preserving important life events, especially the good ones, feel almost like a responsibility we have to future generations. There are also psychological reasons for the scrapbooking phenomenon.

- **Create order out of chaos**—The bag full of "stuff" that you collected on your European holiday can once again see the light of day after forty years of darkness. Bring it out of the basement and set it free.
- **Make the intangible tangible**—Accessing digital photography can be cumbersome when you want to enjoy your wonderful memories, especially if you weren't born with a computer in your face. Liberate

them with a home in your photo album. (If your computer crashes, you will be very happy you did.)
- **Stimulate your senses**—Photos and other pieces of memorabilia can stimulate vision, touch, smell, and hearing. Reliving the really special moments of your life brings great satisfaction at any age.
- **Enjoy selective memory**—only include the "best" of the event. Why relive the trauma that tends to stalk many a momentous occasion? (Unless there is the potential byproduct of bribery or revenge, then go for it.)

Okay, I admit it—since I started looking into the phenomenon of scrapbooking, my research has converted me. I have seen the light beaming from those neatly arranged pages in my friends's albums (she would say "scrapbooks"). Now all I need is the time to get a little scrappy.

A Brief Diversion

 Once all of your mess is captured and tamed, it can be stored in new spaces found by expanding vertical storage either in new digs or your existing nest.

FEELING COCKY?
A Reason to Crow

SUMMER MEANS State Fair time, and that means that the exotic chickens (with better hair-dos than we have) will be strutting around, looking gorgeous. One of the highlights of the hot, stinky, dirty, calorie-infested fair is the much anticipated viewing of these Hedda Hopper look-alikes.

"How is this dangerous?" you ask the team here at Aging but DANGEROUS (feeling cocksure that you have us on this one). "How is a beautiful Paduan or Sultan or Crevecoeur chicken dangerous?" Because more and more people are making pets out of these **magnificent creatures.** Chickens in the house? That sounds plenty dangerous to us.

When I was in grade school, my sister and I got chickens for Easter one year. Very quickly they were transported to my grandparents' farm, where they turned from little yellow pooping fur balls into magnificent large red hens (still pooping randomly, however). For some bizarre reason (I am sure it was my sister's idea), we named them all Wilber. We found that if we moved very quickly, we could nab a Wilber and carry it around, kind of like a dog. No tricks, however.

One by one, the Wilbers began to disappear. Years later, I wondered if there was any correlation between vanishing Wilbers and the chicken dinners that accompanied our visits. *Should I have suspected fowl play?*

If you visit www.urbanchicken.org, you will be amazed at the information and options offered to the urban chicken owner. These pets are smart, they can be real characters, and they lay eggs—sounds like a good companion to us. *The pooping thing is our only concern.*

At Aging But DANGEROUS, we encourage women to step out of the norm and push themselves to be a little off the wall, go a little crazy, be a little dangerous, think outside the coop. So, if you have ever had any desire to form a closer bond with a fowl that is all decked out for the Kentucky Derby—don't be a chicken. Own one!

A Brief Diversion

 These chickens are yard accessories that you can admire for their beauty and unique personality. If you realized that you have truly laid an egg concerning this investment, there is always Sunday dinner.

MOVIN' ON

WHEN JEAN'S HUSBAND Mike needed help moving their stuff from one storage shed to another, he asked if we would help. Yeah, right—this could be **dangerous**. Do we look like our names are Mayflower?

Bad backs and all, we headed to storage unit number one and loaded the first huge cart full of what Mike called "indescribable" treasures. Just as I was assuring Jean that I knew how to steer the Jurassic cart, I slightly over-compensated on a turn and nicked the corner of a wall. Rakes, brooms, and mops flew. We laughed so hard we almost wet our pants. (Actually, Jean did!)

Mike was not impressed or compassionate. He had that, "Oh crap, we'll never get this done" look on his face. Buzzkill!

Yet we finished the day in fine shape, mission accomplished. The next morning, Mike asked Jean to please try and find the truck that he was sure had hit him the previous day (pansy). Jean and I felt great. Why? Here are a few tried and true lifting tips that we think saved us and are worth repeating. (*These are also good to bear in mind when picking up grandkids, too.*)

- We squared up with the boxes we were lifting and got as close as we could.
- We got a good grip before the actual lift.
- We used our bent legs and our arms, *NOT OUR BACKS*.
- We looked up toward the ceiling before we lifted.
- We didn't arch our backs, and we kept the load close to our bodies.
- We stayed hydrated.
- We laughed frequently and for no good reason.
- We (she) made a pledge to pitch most of the crap that we had just moved. (Praise the Lord!)

We made the afternoon fun and celebrated our accomplishment with margaritas. *Maybe that is the truck that Mike was looking for.*

A CLASSIC RE-BIRTH—JUST LIKE US

ONE OF MY FAVORITE days of each year is the vernal equinox, when the length of our days becomes equal with the length of night (and, going forward, grows even longer). Rejuvenation and rebirth are everywhere during that time. But self-rejuvenation and rebirth are not seasonal. What is **your** rejuvenation project? I know—you like yourself just the way you are. *Really?* **Exactly** the way you are?

We change, the world changes, and part of our Aging But DANGEROUS philosophy is to stay in step with the universe. Ever-changing knowledge feeds the soul. In many cases our automobiles and our homes get more maintenance than our bodies (I call mine my container) or our brains. Just because you have been doing something for years doesn't mean that there shouldn't be a little upgrade in your future.

Let's take ice cream—frozen guilt. After decades of bovine domination, enter the free-range goats—a rebirth of sorts. When made from goat's milk, this delicacy contains about half the fat of the old familiar standby, has more calcium, magnesium, and potassium, and contains no antibiotics or growth hormones. Check it out www.laloos.com: it's udderly delicious!

How about M&Ms®? Talk about a tired but familiar old standard getting a little update! New colors like silver, "electric green," and pearl have pumped new life into this beloved treat. Custom design your own signature decadence. M&M Premiums have transformed from the inside out—always an admirable exercise. www.mms.com

And if there is any doubt left that you can teach an old dog how to "glam up," enter the new, glamorous, glitter-infused, scented, multi-shaded, glow-in-the-dark crayon. Crayola sensed that, after a century, they might need a little physical and emotional lift. We concur—wouldn't we all? www.crayola.com

Most importantly, spiffing up from the inside out will do what no other cosmetic or external perk can ever do.

Find *just one thing* about the way your brain works that you would like to re-birth, and replace it with a positive, inspirational saying or thought. Since ninety-five percent of what we do is from habit, you *can* reprogram your brain. My spring mantra is "love never fails." When I get irritated with the numerous people who know how to push my buttons, I pause, smile, and think, "Love never fails." Result? Temporary relief from the urge to deck somebody. It's as gratifying as spring flowers.

Try enhancing your color, reducing your fat, or sweetening your existence. A snazzier, updated you, in any season, will bring you great joy! You'll feel almost as yummy as that ice cream.

WHAT YOU "SEE" IS WHAT YOU GET!

THE POWER OF THE MIND is a mysterious and amazing thing. It is a vast, sparsely-explored frontier capable of accomplishing infinite tasks. My focus of late has been on "visualization." This is the power to use your imagination to create a clear vision in your mind of what you want (or think you want)—from a physical thing like a new BMW or a new apartment to an emotional state such as self-confidence—and getting it! Visualization as a means to accomplish a goal is not a new concept. *The Secret* (a best-selling 2006 self-help book written by Rhonda Byrne) is based on the law of attraction and claims that positive thinking can create life-changing results such as increased happiness, health, and wealth. It is not really a secret! Yet the power of using the energy of the mind to manifest our dreams certainly wasn't something we understood or embraced during my formative childhood years. Back then, it was called "daydreaming," and grownups did not hold it in particularly high regard.

Our Perception IS Our Reality. What we didn't know about Shakti Gawain, the dynamic author and leader in the field of personal development beginning in the late-1970s, was that she would make "creative visualization" a household word. Or that she would popularize the concept of intuitive guidance in the 1980s. How right on she was. Her inspirational message is, "To use creative visualization, it is not necessary to believe in any metaphysical or spiritual ideas, though you must be willing to entertain concepts as being possible. The only thing necessary is that you have the desire..." Now *that's* something I know a lot about—desire.

For all of us Boomers who have ever felt doomed by destiny or deluged by the feeling that, as we age, we control very little, visualization is empowering. It gives us hope and sanity during the dark days when there seems to be no light at the end of the tunnel (or the dwindling bank balance). The idea that we have some influence on what happens next in our lives—wow, what a concept!

Despite having taken different spiritual paths, one of us through prayer, one through meditation, Jean and I have both been able to harness an ability to form a clear picture of what we would like to bring into our lives and to hold that image until it becomes a reality. How the heck do you think Aging But DANGEROUS happened?

If you are interested in changing your life or in knowing more about this subject, go back to basics—the foundation, if you will—of a very trendy yet effective skill. Visit www.shaktigawain.com to learn more about creative visualization.

The idea that our minds control our reality may seem like an episode of Rod Serling's *Twilight Zone*, but visualization has been a powerful force in both of our lives, and it can be a GR*E*AT tool for turning your dreams into reality. Wouldn't you look great in that _____ [fill in the blank with *your* desire]?

> ### A Brief Diversion
>
> - Visualize those new digs you would love to occupy *only* if you are truly prepared to relocate. Or, as my mom says, "Be careful what you wish or pray for, because you'll probably get it."
> - "You don't get to choose how you're going to die or when. You can only decide how you're going to live. Now."—*Joan Baez*

DIRTY LITTLE SECRETS

GETTING TRASHED

CO_2-

I LIKE TALKING TRASH, but it just doesn't have the naughty little edge that it used to. (Sorry!) These days, "talking trash" means reducing your carbon footprint and helping the world be a cleaner, safer, healthier place to live—for us and our offspring. We need trash talk and then *action*.

For example, on a daily basis, Tiffany Threadgould and her company RePlay-Ground live the idea of "trash to treasure." They reincarnate garbage into usable products. Although this initially may seem to be a disgusting and possibly *dangerous* concept, she really has some good ideas. Make a paper-tube fruit bowl for your kitchen or dining area: it's a great way to add an accent color and could be fabulous (and what a hoot of a gift idea for the financially strapped). Visit www.replay-ground.com for some great info, as well as some highly tricked-out project suggestions.

And spread the word about using the items you already have instead of buying new—don't let it be just *your* trashy little secret.

OFF THE WALL GARDENS

WHEN YOU ARRIVE at the human mile marker stamped 50+, defying gravity becomes painfully more difficult. Oh!—I bet you were thinking of body parts. Well, that too, but gravity-denial doesn't have to be difficult when it comes to gardens.

As we move into more compact living spaces, we are faced with dwindling garden space in which to express our "agrarian side." To remove a gardener from her turf is downright cruel and potentially dangerous. I know what you once said about "not wanting the responsibility of a big yard," but if you have used the soil as a grounding element in your life, then chances are your withdrawal from indulging in terra firma will be fierce.

Thank goodness someone has invented Woolly Pocket Wally containers, which make vertical garden spaces an attainable fantasy. Well-known landscape designer Jamie Durie calls them "the poor man's version" of a vertical garden. Prices start at about $40.

My first introduction to these wonderful little pockets of recycled plastic was in Madrid, Spain, in September 2009. Lush and colorful plants climbed four stories into the air to connect seamlessly with the soft blue sky. It was breathtaking. Upon digging into the thick green foliage, I found what I thought to be wool containers applied to the side of a building. This product was worth a little research.

When you first plant them, your soon-to-be-prolific planters look a little like re-assigned long underwear from pioneer days. But soon your Woolly Wallys will be sprouting color and hues of green that will knock your own wooly little socks off.

For information on installation, picking the right soil, choosing the perfect plants or just tracking Wally down, go to www.woollypocket.com/qa.php.

The Aging But DANGEROUS crew gives this soft yet edgy product a double green thumbs up.

THE GRASS IS ALWAYS GREENER...

GROWING "GREEN" GRASS is somewhat of an oxymoron, since most of us use pesticides and synthetic nitrogen to accomplish that end—and that truly *is **dangerous**. At Harvard they switched their lawn care to organic methods* like compost and compost tea (the thought makes me want to spit), and the results have been stunning. The microbes that now feed the grass have turned it healthy, lush, and truly green naturally—and that is wise.

For more information, go to: www.uos.harvard.edu/fmo/landscape/organiclandscaping. The grass truly is greener on their side of the fence.

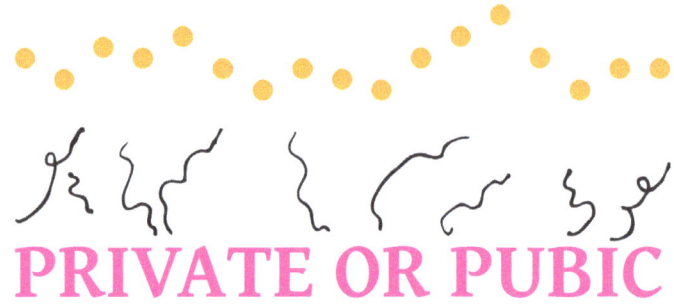

PRIVATE OR PUBIC

SEVERAL YEARS AGO, my mom told me that at some point during the aging process all of one's pubic hair falls out. I had never heard that—I was appalled. Having just gone through the required bathing suit prep necessary for a warm-weather vacation (remember the scene from the movie *Sex in the City?* It can get really disgusting sans prep), I may be ready to molt. And for those of you who have inquired about the source of those wicked chin hairs... we may have found the answer.

A Brief Diversion

 Don't you wish there was something constructive we could do with pubic hair. How about throw pillows? Any other ideas?

UPON REFLECTION

BIGGER IS BETTER when it comes to mirrors and faces. Magnification helps you deal with issues created by applying makeup that regular mirrors won't even show. If you take care of challenges in "the bigger picture," the overall outcome improves greatly. Yes, at first it is terrifying to look at those Jurassic features looking back at you. Spielberg himself might shudder. Get over it!

Do your best makeup work at this scale (5x, 7x; I am up to 10x), and when you look in a "real" mirror, you will gasp, "Is that the prom queen? Oh, no… it's me!"

WHEN YOU'RE HOT, YOU'RE HOT

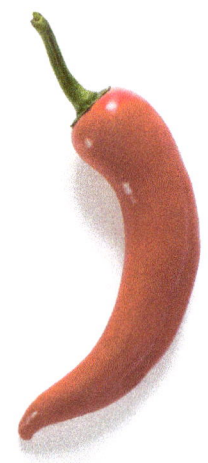

SEVERAL YEARS AGO, we did a survey asking women we knew what we thought was a serious question: *"When was the last time you felt hot?"* (Hot as in sexy; not flashes.) Replies ranged from "not recently" to "never." *Never?* We were amazed.

Then we read an article about a writer who felt she didn't have "sexy-making instincts." She didn't say it exactly that way; we are taking the liberty of summarizing. A photo of her revealed much of the problem. She looked like someone had knitted her. She was over-the-top homespun. One of her colleagues suggested that she should put some effort into appearing like she hadn't just stepped off a package of cookies (like something the Keebler elves might have conjured up).

The next photo was amazing: hair down, skirt appropriately short (just at the knee) and fitted, heeled shoes. She was definitely looking "hot" and, by her own admission, felt similarly. Not looking hot was a choice she had made historically. She chose to dumb-down her full potential because she was more comfortable that way.

Here is our point: It is *sooo* easy to get into the rut of **not** putting our full effort into **looking great**, and **feeling great**, which often go hand in hand. With every season, we have many opportunities to take our appearance, hence our attitude, up a notch.

Wear a nice skirt (try Target) to replace those uniform-ish pants.

Sport a stylish, flattering shirt that has a little punch: maybe fitted; maybe with the opportunity to show a little cleavage.

Shoes are designed to give you both comfort and style these days. Go for a slightly higher heel, or do a color that rocks your ensemble.

Current jewelry trends make it easy to get mileage from your accessories; just glom on everything in your jewelry box that matches or not. A great scarf, a wonderful bag—all are great weapons of mass construction.

Why are makeover shows so popular? Because it is as exciting to see others bloom as it is to see ourselves bloom. We hear the same words spoken over and over by those recycled souls: "I *feel* so good about myself." That's what it is all about!

In *Elle* magazine recently, we read these wonderful words: "Some recent shifts in fashion transcend age. It's not our job to tell a sixty-four-year-old woman who looks fabulous in a pair of platforms that she can't wear them because she's too old. If you look great, you should be able to celebrate and wear the things you love." Hallelujah!!

Go for it! When someone said, "You reap what you sow," do you think they really meant "sew"? We should have known that they were talking about fashion.

A Brief Diversion

- *InStyle* magazine stated, "We hail Helen Mirren's ubiquity, because it serves a more triumphant purpose—a constant reminder that women can not only be gifted, witty, and charming after… say, sixty-two, but also ridiculously sexy." Now, at sixty-six, she has been voted Best Body of the Year by LA Fitness.

- "You can take no credit for beauty at sixteen. But if you are beautiful at sixty, it will be your soul's own doing."—Marie Stopes

- Sexiness is not horniness, writes Meghan Daum for *Allure*. "There is a sizable, if nuanced, distinction... we might say that sexiness is to horniness as Epicureanism is to hunger." She declares that sexiness transcends age and is as much about posture and vocal intonation as it is about cleavage or skirt length or the dimensions of our posteriors. "Feeling sexy is, at its root, about owning ourselves. It's being at home in our own skins. No wonder it is so damn elusive."

- Remember, our goal is to be the best we can with what we have. Mayo Clinic says, "Don't obsess about not being perfect" (none of us are). It's unhealthy and leads to serious illnesses, even death.

DEFINE SEXY

"EVERY WOMAN WANTS to feel sexy." It seems we've run across that remark way too frequently of late *not* to question its validity. *We disagree!*

In the *New York Times*, on *CBS Sunday Morning*, and in most magazines, this sneaky pseudo-edict floats by unceremoniously. Are we being brainwashed? At fifty years of age and older, how often do you feel sexy? Are they confusing sensual or pretty with sexy? What constitutes sexy? How close are sexy and sexual?

Our research about feeling sexy produced an unnerving number of photographs of women exposing most of their unusually large breasts by wearing ridiculously low-cut attire. Don't get us wrong: we love the low-cut, cleavage-enhanced image of ourselves. But is flashing the masses the same as feeling sexy? Our Aging But DANGEROUS crew thinks not.

Feeling sexy or sensual or pretty comes first from inside. Jefferson Airplane nails it when they sing, "Pretty As You Feel."

"You're only pretty as you feel/Only pretty as you feel inside."

It's all about the "head" thing again—it always is. What we perceive we are—we are.

What has helped me feel sexy (and sensual), fashionably forward, and probably turn a few heads (albeit gray-haired heads) are the following tweaks you can easily accomplish:

- **Shoes:** A new pair of comfortable, sexy shoes (this is not an oxymoron) with as high a heel as you can handle. They do exist.
- **Posture:** Posture is huge; if we can keep our shoulder blades in our back pockets and stand erect, we can knock five years off our bodies in a fraction of a second.
- **Eye makeup:** Have a trained makeup artist (found at department stores) give your eyes a new look. Make it clear up front that you are experimenting and may or may not buy product. Bobby Brown at Hall's in Kansas City (Susan, to be exact) gave my

eyes a new look several years ago. That has made a really positive impact on my self-image.
- **Hair style:** Get a good professional to give you an honest evaluation. My ninety-year-old mom still looks fantastic and, periodically, still sexy because she keeps her hair current with the times. (Thank goodness she's over her orange hair phase. That was a tough one.)
- **Fragrance:** Nothing says "I'm sexy" like smelling great. Not too much "great," however—the older we get, the less we can smell. Don't knock people over! Check with a friend to see if you are asphyxiating her.

You probably know your own hot buttons—there are multitudes of them. What makes *you* feel great about yourself? New lingerie? A pedicure? Yoga? Tell yourself how awesome you are, resurrect those flirting skills from a few years back, and, most importantly, have a blast!

If feeling sexy (or, God forbid, more sexual) isn't your gig, take a look at the list above anyway. There is no downside to enhancing the you that you have (I hope) grown to love. (But keep your breasts *inside* your shirt; flashing is illegal!)

Refer to the following links for more hot information:

http://bestofeverythingafter50.com/tag/feeling-invisible-after-50/

http://www.babyboomers-lifes-pleasures.com/feel-sexier.html

OVER-EXPOSURE

MANY YEARS AGO, I sat on a topless beach in the Bahamas with a group of women and actually wrote a mission statement—one that is as profound and right-on today as it was when my breasts were less gravitized. My deeply-embedded Puritan genes made me see that event as "brazen" and "risky."

Then, years later, I headed to Mexico, planning to sun my fit little sixty-plus-year-old body on a topless beach (the half Monty). I was apprehensive. Why? Bodies are bodies—right? Was I squeamish about this because my svelteness wasn't that of a twenty-year-old? Was this an issue of self-acceptance? I was asking myself, "Why didn't I get that breast lift when I had the money?" Was this my perfectionist angst being totally unrealistic? I will report back to you—this felt DANGEROUS! (But oh-so-exciting.)

Later... Sparkling, azure water lapped the sun-soaked beach of Isla Mujeres. I was ready to make my brazen, topless debut in Mexico. First, I stealthily separated myself from my friends, then I scouted out areas with the least congestion. I innocently meandered over to a yellow chaise lounge chair and daintily sat down then reclined. Once I became totally prone, I released the clasp on the back of my bathing suit top and *ta-da*! Topless! This felt great, free, liberating! I was beyond comfortable. I planned to relax while tanning my milky white breasts to a toasty bronze. I had done it—I felt quite accomplished.

Then he appeared—first I felt his shadow then the voice. "Excuse me, ma'am, these are rental chairs."

Crap, how would I know? Where was the sign?

"How much," I asked (not having planned on exposed nipple negotiations).

"Fifteen dollars," he answered. As happy and content as I felt lying unencumbered on that beautiful, sun-drenched beach, the economics just weren't there.

When I considered that it would take very little time to fry my pale mammaries (half an hour or so), I caved. "Sorry," I said. "I'll move." I felt as if people were staring. Discomfort mixed with a little embarrassment replaced my tranquility. Now I just felt conspicuous. My attempt to casually put the girls back in the hammock were futile. I finally had to flip to my stomach to get them to come out from under my armpits and be harnessed.

That's it—a flash of euphoria followed by an awkward squirming that may have resembled a worm on hot concrete. It was heartbreaking. I was briefly Aging But DANGEROUS to my fullest capacity. And maybe that's the moral: staying abreast of your fantasies doesn't mean you're *always* going to end up feeling like a boob!

A Brief Diversion

Adventureswithben.com suggests the following for your first visit to a nude (or topless) beach.

- Don't Arrive Naked—It could be too frightening.
- Go with a Trusted Friend—Remember, if you're gettin' naked, so's your friend
- Leave the Camera at Home—It's rude.
- Don't Stare—Yes, sometimes you may want to sneak a peek. So just wear sunglasses when you do it. Everyone else does.
- Bring Suntan Lotion and Use it *EVERYWHERE*! Need I say more? (Don't forget: you've been warned.)
- Act Normal—What do people at a nude beach do? The same thing people do at a regular beach.

Lesson: Nude (or topless) beaches aren't gross. Nor are they dirty. They are just like other beaches but with a lot more skin. Love yourself and your body. You deserve it!

HAIR-RAISING!

SEVERAL YEARS AGO, I lost the stylist with whom I had maintained an eighteen-year professional relationship. Shortly after that, I started my new journey with a young thing at the same salon. Then I received a brief letter in the mail from her stating, "I feel this is not a good match, and I can no longer be your stylist." I had been fired! She did not want to do my hair—the nerve! Could she actually do that?

Oh, the pain of rejection. My emotions ran the gamut from rage to shame, humiliation to disgrace. Wounded, bitter, and potentially scarred for life, I finally moved on.

Flash four years forward. My sister finds another new young thing in Kansas City to highlight her hair. She articulates to a fault *exactly* what she wants him to do. She is kind, friendly, and respectful, but the pressure is palpable—she knows what she wants, and he knows that she knows exactly what she wants. There are re-dos. Then her letter arrived.

Misery does love company... as does embarrassment, mortification, and irritation. Could this be genetic? And why do I smile every time I think of *her* letter?

The moral here is not to take your stylist for granted. Behave and be mindful not to be annoying. You may be closer than you think to having your relationship end up in the salon trash with that pile of hair your stylist just removed from your own head.

A Brief Diversion

- Lily Tomlin about hairstyling: "If truth is beauty, how come no one has their hair done in the library?"
- According to Rejuvenation Salon & Spa in Tacoma, Washington, most salons don't "...discriminate against the way you dress, talk, look, or the way you smell. One of our *BIGGEST* refusals in a salon is for head lice." (*Creepy crawlers we did not have.*)
- Dale Alexander wrote in "Five Signs It's Time to Fire Your Client" that "showing up late for appointments, talking on the phone during a service, reading or texting during a service, telling a stylist how to do his job, and being disrespectful" are all grounds for a sanctimonious salon split-up.

GOT BALLS?

WORD ON THE STREET several years ago was that three crazy guys were throwing naked ping pong parties in the Tribeca neighborhood of New York City. We were stunned. Now we get it: who would talk about people playing ping pong with clothes on? We have been doing that for years (old news)—but naked: *that's* quite a different story. How much more *dangerous* can you get than a couple of 50+ men and women slamming a little white ball at body parts that haven't seen the light of day (or night) in public in decades, maybe never?

You can rest easy, however, because "they" (the promoters) don't really want "us" anyway. Bud Light and other sponsors are aiming for the younger set and hoping that table tennis (as we are now calling it) will be "the next poker." ESPN even airs tournaments these days.

If this sounds like your shtick (or paddle), then head for N.Y.C. to visit SPiN, a Manhattan club dedicated solely to table tennis. Susan Sarandon, Todd Oldham, and several other undisclosed celebrity-types have backed this trendy new establishment that, initially, had a VIP lounge but no kitchen or liquor license. Odd, but the club did quite well sans nourishment or legal imbibing. Star power has great reach.

This seems to be a case of "acting un-cool inevitably becomes kind of, well, cool," says Mitchell Seidenfeld, a two-time Paralympic gold medalist, member of the U.S. Paralympic team, and participant in the ESPN ping pong gig (officially called the HardBat Classic). That's probably why celebrities like Matthew Broderick, Ed Norton, and Judah Fiedlander patronize SPiN: all these (young) actors are known for embracing their own oddball ways.

We at Aging But DANGEROUS think that resurrecting this sport will serve us all well. Ping pong can be played at any level, by any gender of any age. Be competitive *and fun!*

When it comes to that little white ball, you can block it, chop it, drop it, kill it, or lob it. Nuances and techniques of the game basically remain the same. But *please*, for goodness sake, try to keep your clothes on!

STAND UP STRAIGHT

"**PUT YOUR SHOULDER** blades in your back pockets," a friend said to me recently while walking. Once I did that, I felt like Marilyn Monroe: my breasts elevated several inches from their previous position.

Posture is one of those ongoing challenges that seems to be more difficult with every year. *Natural News* magazine quotes Nobel Prize-recipient Dr. Roger Sperry as saying that bad posture is "a modern day health epidemic." If we stand up straight, our lungs fill with more air, which oxygenates our blood. Our organs work better, our backs don't hurt as much, depression lessens and we actually look and feel younger and more fit. (That is, more attractive.)

The Kellogg School of Management at Northwestern University found that "posture had a strong effect in making a person think and act in a more powerful way." Aging But DANGEROUS feels there is a correlation between standing up straight and tall and having the strength to expand your boundaries to areas you have previously only dreamed about. So get those shoulders up, back, and down—*pronto*!

My new ploy is to put Post-It notes at every turn (front door, bathroom mirror, closet door, etc.) with gentle, humorous reminders to try and touch those shoulder blades together (preferably behind me) as often as I can.

Who knew that what Marilyn Monroe was teaching us back in the '50s was actually healthy?

All the following links will inspire you to suck that gut in and stick that chest out no matter how tired you feel.

http://www.bhg.com/health-family/fitness/workouts-programs/exercises-to-improve-your-posture/

http://www.oprah.com/health/Back-Posture-Help-Exercises-to-Stand-Up-Straight

http://www.naturalnews.com/030956_posture_health.html

http://www.kellogg.northwestern.edu/News_Articles/2011/powerful-posture.aspx

THE EYES HAVE IT!
A Brow-Beating

EYEBROWS CAN BE TRICKY. Somehow, I have this St. Louis Arch thing going on with my eyebrows, and I don't even know how it happened. It just evolved. My sis has Tallulah Bankhead/Marlene Dietrich brows. All she needs is a cigarette holder, more hair, and voila! Tallulah. Jean's brow evolves by the moment.

My "arch" revelation inspired me to seek out the perfect brow... as illustrated in these graphics. Brow proportions are all a geometrical diagram that is based on the side of the nose. Use an eyebrow pencil to map your coordinates.

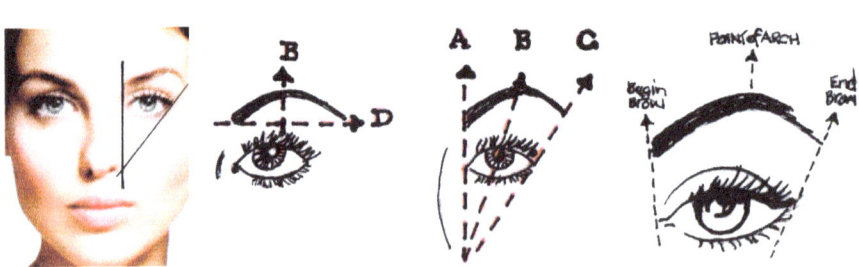

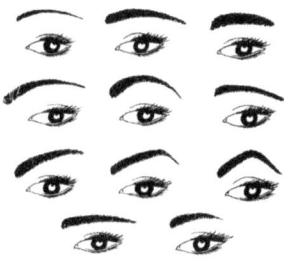

Frustration set in when the hair that used to be in my eyebrows and other, more private areas migrated to my chin. Tattooing my brows in place seemed like a feasible option but hurt like hell. Transplants were another approach to thickening my waning brow, but it seems that the hair they take from the back of your scalp to put into your eyebrow doesn't actually know that it is now on your face, and grows accordingly. That's spooky.

While Frida Kahlo sported the unibrow as a sign of her individuality and female strength, women in Iran use an "ungroomed" brow as a sign of virginity. (Good luck with that one, Suzanne.)

Brows have acted as significant historical markers. In the 1940s and '50s, women wore almost no brow. (Were they differentiating themselves from men after the war?) The '60s androgynous brow (think Brooke Shields, although she came later) was part of what were hairy times in **many** respects. In the '80s (Brooke notwithstanding), we were back to thin and perfectly groomed (maybe a power thing—self obsession?). The '90s saw a more natural, environmentally friendly "green" brow. Go figure.

Blink Eyebrow Bar in London actually asks people, "What do they want out of their eyebrows?" *Really?* Who thinks about this?

Check out your brows, and see if they meet these specifications. Are you more *"aging"* or more *"dangerous"*? Then look at our charts and diagrams, and go to work. Good cosmetic aids will make this endeavor much more successful. Seek counsel from the pros wherever high quality cosmetics are sold. (You don't have to buy; just ask questions.) Whether you are high brow or low brow, this exercise can't hurt. Don't be like me and end up with that St. Louis downtown skyline look.

A Brief Diversion

- Remember, as you groom your brows to perfection: *you pluck a chicken, you tweeze a brow.*

- *EASY ON THE EYES!* During allergy season the temptation to rub your eyes is excruciating—*don't!* A plastic surgeon told me once (the same one that "did" my eyes) that *"rubbing your eyes will create wrinkles and bags faster than anything else."* When women cry, they should *blot* the tears. When your eyes itch so badly that clawing them out of their sockets actually sounds like a good idea, use a simple saline eyewash (you can buy that or make it). When putting on eye makeup or taking it off, be *gentle*—always merely pat the eye area. And when you *must* scratch, use a Q-tip.

TOE TO TOE

EXPOSING MY TOES at each year's inaugural flip-flop event is one of my favorite pastimes. What a blissful happening: unencumbered metatarsals freed from confinement to move around as they wish and live their oxygenated summer life—oh, joy! My pedicure is scheduled.

Simultaneously, as I fantasize about my beautifully-groomed phalanges, flowers are blooming, trees are budding, and birds are having sex everywhere I look. (Yes, I'm a "peeping" Tom.) We hear so much about renewal and rebirth as warm weather begins to penetrate our chilled bones.

We think aging has many similarities. As Agatha Christie said in her autobiography, published in 1977, "I have enjoyed greatly the **second blooming** that comes when you finish the life of the emotions and of personal relations; and suddenly find—at the age of fifty, say—that a whole **new life** has opened before you, filled with things you can think about, study, or read about … It is as if a fresh sap of ideas and thoughts was rising in you."

Whether your thoughts turn toward religious connotations of the spring season or the more pragmatic notions of cleaning and rebuilding your nest, many of us seem to struggle with a cleansing question: what do we need to let go of?

The "second bloom" is much fuller and more luscious when proper pruning has occurred.

Find one betrayal to let go of, one crushed emotion to release. Stop telling that same story of disappointment over and over again—renew! Or, as Dolly Parton so eloquently put it, "get off that cross, somebody else needs the wood." Make room for the new blossoms, followed by the plentiful fruit that will now have room to thrive. We at Aging But DANGEROUS are working on our own catharsis so as to fully take advantage of the soft, spring breezes tickling our newly-polished toes, the warmth of the sun that bathes us in soft rays, and the gentle rains that will nourish us and our surroundings through this evolution. We are trying to sprout, to flower as we age, to blossom as we mature.

Let's just pray that my soul can look as good as my toes.

STARVING – OR DOES IT JUST LOOK THAT WAY?

BLUBBER. THAT IS the first word that comes to my mind. It has begun to surround my midsection. Much like hot fudge flows over a large scoop of Häagen-Dazs® ice cream (see, there I go!), it adheres to my body, and we become one. I'm disgusted with myself! In years gone by, I could make a Thin Mint Girl Scout cookie last for two meals. Now, I consume an entire sleeve in one sitting.

A convergence of circumstances has occurred, the results of which are most evident around my middle.

My metabolism has slowed, and, after years of running, my knees begged to retire so I granted them mercy! My cravings have turned to sugar, my drug of choice. Meanwhile, the "no thank you" part of my brain has been destroyed by some sinister plot to fatten me up.

Even more frustrating, Jean has just lost fifteen pounds on her Aging But DANGEROUS 20# Club Diet. She smugly watches me tie on the feedbag that has led to my mid-section metamorphosis. She is not hungry, is thinner than I have seen her in years, and feels fabulous. Why do I even like this woman? This predicament is *so* annoying!

If I sound "hangry," I shouldn't, because I'm well fed, but I'm oh-so-frustrated. If Jean's decreasing waistline wasn't enough to irritate me, the fact that I actually ripped a zipper out of a pair of leather pants last week has put me over the edge. (I attempted to bend over after a wonderfully delicious pail-size bowl of carrot and ginger soup.) Where is that portion control? I surrender!

Today I am joining the 20# Club, even if I only need to lose ten pounds. If Jean and millions of others can do it, I can do it, too! I need support! I need a plan! I need new tools, and I need a healthier body, a new attitude, and guidance. Jean assures me she is deliciously thrilled with all of the benefits of the 20# Club.

If you want to join me on this scrumptious journey to blubber elimination, contact that skinny business partner of mine through our website. I'm planning on being fed a buffet of healthy behaviors that will be the best accessory I could ever invest in. *Bon appetit!*

To be fed guidance, information and cheerleading, go to: www.agingbutdangerous.com and click on 20# Club.

DON'T
BE
A
BOOB!

HEAVY LIFTING?

RECENTLY WE DISCOVERED a product called Cleavage Cupcakes. These soft, comfortable silicone inserts provide excellent push-up power and oomph. If you're not filling out your favorite sweater the way you used to, give these a try. (Although, according to the docs, there is no way short of surgery to tighten and lift breasts that sag.) Find them here:

http://www.herlook.com/cleavagecupcakes.html?gclid=CLSg5tXyxpoCFRk_awodTgqd3A

Although we at Aging But DANGEROUS have not opted for surgery (yet!), we did some research into it and found out that breast lift surgery ("mastopexy," to be exact) is actually pretty common. According to the American Society of Plastic Surgeons (ASPS), breast lifts increased by 70% from 2000 to 2014. About twice the increase of breast implants. In 2013 there were 90,006 lifts in the US, in 2014there were 92,740. The women who gain the best results from this type of surgery have smaller breasts—the "lift" lasts longer when there is not so much to weigh them down.

According to the ASPS web site, based on their statistics and data, the average cost for a breast lift in 2014 was $4,377. According to RealSelf.com, in 2012, in the Twin Cities, a breast lift ranged from $6,000 to $8,000 without implants. Implants add around $1,000 for saline and $1,700 for silicone. The cost is based on the experience of the surgeon, the type of procedure, and the geographic area. Costs may also include anesthesia, hospital or surgical facility, medical tests, post-surgery garments, post-surgery prescriptions, and the surgeon's fee.

Many women go for the full Monty and get breast lifts combined with breast implants, for a complete package that not only increases their bust size but also maintains their new, younger-looking breast shape for a longer time.

Or you can do what I did for my fortieth high school class reunion. When my dress didn't fit quite the way I had anticipated, I stuck running socks in the bottom of my bra to create the cleavage that I so badly needed. Not the most glamorous solution—but definitely dangerous. A totally new meaning for "sock it to me."

NOT A PERFECT PAIR

FRUIT OF THE LOOM now has a bra for lop-sided women (of whom we know many). "Pick Your Perfect Pair" lets you purchase separate cup sizes and then snap them together in the front to make your perfect-fitting lop-sided bra. If there isn't an entire cup size difference in your catawampusness, you can buy their "Exactly" size for one side—let's say a true B cup—and their "Just About" size (with extra padding) for the other side. That is like a B minus or A plus—not quite a full B. Now you can make *both* the twins happy with one garment!

Just in case your girth size fluctuates substantially, they have given us five rows of hooks to choose from in the back. There is a lot of adjustment potential in five rows of hooks.

Better yet, this bra is truly affordable at $5 per cup. A cup of cappuccino may cost you a fortune these days, but this unique approach to holding up the girls will leave you with money to spare, especially when compared to other uplifting alternatives.

http://www.pickyourperfectpairbras.com/

KEEPING ABREAST

SAGGING BREASTS SUCK. But there are far worse issues. Losing a breast used to be one of my biggest fears. It's one that many women share. But now that two of our very close friends have survived the removal of a breast and seem to be very content with their own physicality, our fears have dissipated. One chose reconstruction and one chose to wear a prosthesis. In both cases, the "rookie" breast is much better looking than the "veteran" breast. Oh, the miracles of technology.

Another friend had both her breasts removed when she was only forty-two. She referred to herself as *"the young and the breastless." What a great attitude*!

Virginia Piper Breast Center at Abbott Northwestern Hospital in Minneapolis told us that for years, health insurance payed for breast forms and bras for women who had mastectomies and lumpectomies, whether the procedure was done recently or preformed many years ago. (Depending on your insurance and your coverage that resource may no longer be available.) As of 2015, the American Cancer Society is a trusted resource to which you can turn. Call 1-800-227-2345 and they will check to see what your best course of action is based on your geographic location. Funds seem to come and go and vary based on your geography. Open twenty-four hours a day, seven days a week, they will work with you to help you obtain breast forms and bras, and I'm sure address myriad other questions or concerns with which you might be dealing.

Sadly, every woman's chances for getting breast cancer increase with age. That is our **mega message**. Women's risk of breast cancer, by age:

- By age 30 – 1 in 2,525
- By age 40 – 1 in 217
- By age 50 – 1 in 50
- By age 60 – 1 in 24
- By age 70 – 1 in 14

Medical News Today stated that, in the UK, eighty percent of breast cancer cases are in women over fifty. That is four out of five cases. In the U.S., "Women age 65 and older constitute half of new breast cancer patients each year, and the number of older women with breast cancer is forecast to double by 2030, as the baby boomers age." **Be vigilant**! These numbers underscore the importance of keeping up with your yearly mammograms and monthly self-exams, and taking good care of your overall health.

Don't be a boob, take care of those mammaries! We haven't carried them around all these years just to neglect them now that gravity is maneuvering them toward our toes.

A Brief Diversion

My own booby trap... During my junior year in high school, I had invited an older guy (a college freshman) to a formal holiday party sponsored by my sorority. My mom made me a beautiful blue brocade dress to wear, straight cut across the bodice with tiny spaghetti straps. My yet-to-be formed breasts were problematic (yes, I was a late bloomer), as I needed just a hint of cleavage to finish the look of my ensemble. Luckily, we found a long-line bra that had a substantial foam rubber base on which to rest every bit of breast I could conjure up. They sat as if on a little stage. I felt fantastic.

Upon arriving in my driveway just prior to my midnight curfew, we began to "make out." Before I knew it, this "older man," who was clearly more experienced than I was, had shoved his hand down the front of my dress in pursuit of that oh-so-well-placed prize. In this case, truly the booby prize.

Because my breasts were more or less an optical illusion, the sought-after objects were mostly pure foam rubber.

The base of the bra cup flipped upside down under the pressure of his hand. And my right breast, having lost its pedestal, totally disappeared. As if that wasn't humiliating enough, the bra then snapped back, trapping his hand between the giant foam pad and the nothingness of my chest. I was mortified.

He politely extracted his hand with some difficulty. Thank goodness that at that precise moment my parents turned on our unusually annoying porch light.

I never saw him again. This was clearly an example of a bra that shaped not only breasts but destiny, as well.

IF LOOKS COULD KILL

Recapture your juju, your mojo, your spirit, and debunk the mythical norms of how we should look and feel as we age!

"DON'T DRINK AND DRESS"

THAT'S THE ADVICE on the cover of one of my favorite birthday cards. As we age, we don't even need to drink to end up in *dangerous* territory. The occasional food spot (usually front and center), socks or even shoes that don't match, a garment worn backwards or inside-out—all of these and many more dressing faux pas put us in fashion jeopardy.

After dropping my car off for service last week, I realized that I had only buttoned one button of my shirt, the one at mid-breast level. How embarrassing! When I picked my car up yesterday, I wore one of our wonderful and oh-so-succinct Aging But DANGEROUS T-shirts. I hope those words explained everything.

> **A Brief Diversion**
>
> "At each stage of your life, you should show the best and hide the worst."—Veronica Etro, renowned fashion designer and clothing manufacturer

SKIRTING THE ISSUE

SKIRTS HAVE A STORIED history: not only are they the second-oldest garment known to humankind (preceded only by the loincloth), but the term "skirt" was actually used, at one time, as slang for a woman. Try that now, gentlemen!

When I started feeling uncomfortable running around public places in shorts, I decided to skirt up. Jean is entirely content in long pants, but I felt overheated and restricted in slacks. Visions of the classic Marilyn Monroe "skirt ventilation" photo might have deterred me, but I wasn't talking frou-frou like Marilyn's skirt; I was talking more utilitarian. Less fabric, more structure.

When I headed for an outdoor event in summer's hottest weather, I donned a trusty skirt. Having a little air filter up and around my more private areas was cooler and more comfortable than wearing any pants in captivity. Part of that equation is feeling like I look good; a skirt feels more dressed to me.

My favorite skirt is one from Target. It has become a staple in my wardrobe: denim, not expensive, difficult to soil or even abuse, and dresses up or down. The top of it fits like pants—no overflow bulk at the waistline. I live in it!

Whether it is a moderate length, just above the knee (unless your knees could frighten small children), or just below the knee, a skirt lets you move unencumbered by fabric. Or maybe you would feel better in one of those long, gauzy numbers; it's all about personal style.

I have been told lately there is a certain amount of eroticism inherent in wearing a skirt. I somehow must have missed that, but I do get the drift. Feeling great is about your own comfort level and sending whatever message represents you. Maybe that means pushing a little beyond that to which you've grow accustomed. But please, stay away from the loin cloth.

A Brief Diversion

 Design tips are equally valuable and useful, whether they address interiors or fashion. Find your own personal style, maybe with the help of outside counsel, and rock it! You might be amazed at how many people will notice.

JEAN'S JEANS

SEVERAL MONTHS AGO, a miraculous event occurred: Jean bought a pair of jeans. On the Aging But DANGEROUS website, we talk about *danger being a very personal condition.* For Jean, wearing jeans felt dangerous. When we would attend an event together, she would ask what I was wearing. Many times I replied, "Jeans". Her response (which drove me nuts) was, "I don't wear jeans." Fine, deprive yourself of one of the most wonderful inventions of our era—your loss.

Then one day in early summer, as if breaking through some lifelong psychological barrier, she appeared in jeans. Since that day, I have seen her in little else. I hope she takes them off to sleep.

She looks ten years younger, she seems more relaxed, she navigates her surroundings more easily. Her earlier concerns about jeans not flattering her backside are totally unfounded. But the benefits go far beyond ease of movement:

- Jeans as **instant hand wipes**. She is enamored with the opportunity to wipe her hands at will.
- Jeans as **storage**. She loves her newly acquired ability to store stuff in her pockets. When you have never had pockets, this is a real treat.
- Jeans as **wardrobe extender**. She now throws on a cute top, her jeans, and sandals and looks wonderful. One pair of jeans can supplement at least three pair of normal old lady pants.
- Jeans as **environmental benefit**. Wash only when absolutely necessary—this saves water and protects the environment.

Variations in size, price range, color, cut, style, and trim are endless, so finding the perfect fit should not be so difficult—but it can be. *Squidoo* reports that women try on an average of nine pairs of jeans before she finds the right one. So be patient and buy multiples once you've scored. With 450 million pairs sold annually in the U.S., chances are you will find a pair you can truly love. Mid-rise in a more consistent overall color might be great for starters.

If you don't own a pair of jeans, I suggest you go buy one. **The thrills are endless!**

A Brief Diversion

- Denim or fabric in the denim family also makes great, sturdy, and utilitarian upholstery and slip covers. Once I bought a blue denim sofa. It was as versatile as if it were white but required much less maintenance, and I didn't fear drools.

- Dingy or spotted anything is never cool. Clean and crisp always rocks. Forget someone having your backside—have a friend keep an eye on your front side for those pesky spots that mysteriously escape your lips.

- **BOXING?** Laundry is such a drag. But rejoice: soap for intelligent people (who enjoy humor) is (or maybe was) here. We read an article several years ago that Oxydol had upgraded the entire laundry process a notch or two. It was all in the box, literally and figuratively—it was hysterical! It said "Indulge yourself in prose for the fastidious, submit to the squeaky clean wit put forth in 'Not Your Typical Instructions,' and for goodness sakes enjoy conquering your most extreme dirt… not to mention your laundrophobia." This was not your grandmother's laundry soap. Recently when we tried to find this inspiring box we failed. We were sad. The company couldn't even verify it once existed. We love the idea! Okay, Cheer, Tide, Oxy-everything, your opportunity awaits.

BOOGIE ON DOWN
A Casting Call

IN EARLY JANUARY 2010, we posted this challenge on the Aging But DANGEROUS website in preparation for our spring fashion show (We then prayed someone would show up!):

> **TODAY IS THE DAY!** Your chance to get rid of that BIG "BUT" that seems to be lurking in so many of our lives. You know… "I would go try out to be an Aging But DANGEROUS model, BUT…."

GO to the **Aging But DANGEROUS Casting Call** and let your hair down (or pull it up, whichever one looks best). Be a participant, be a cheerleader, or be an observer—but be!

We want women of ALL AGES to come and share in the FUN! Those over 50 (and we card) may try out for a position on our "Kick Ass" Modeling Squad. There will be wonderful resources, products, and information to make a positive impact on your life, no matter what your age—and admission is FREE. Gather those girlfriends, co-workers, or fond acquaintances, and lead them to a unique experience to be enjoyed by all. If you live close to the Twin Cities, are visiting, or just want to hop a plane for the day, DO IT! Can you tell that we are really jazzed?

- —Gift bags for the first 150 people attending both time slots.
- —GREAT door prizes.
- —Healthy endorphins to be released.
- —Live music.
- —A hoot to be had.

You must be 50 or older to **actually** audition; bring ID and head shot.
No experience necessary.
Professional training will be available.
BRING YOUR OWN CHEERING SQUAD!

January 21, 2010 was brutal, roads were icy, and sub-zero temperatures prompted TV weather people to strongly advise that, if you didn't have to leave your nice, safe, warm home, don't!

However, on the 7:00AM news, WCCO-TV, the CBS affiliate in Minneapolis, announced that if you wanted to shake the winter doldrums, you might want to venture out and attend the Aging But DANGEROUS casting call later that morning. They explained all the details and encouraged women to give it a try. Talk about blessings!

MODEL BEHAVIOR

OUR CASTING CALL event was a HUGE success! We met women of all ages and size. Gorgeous women! We saw 60- and 70-plus-year-olds who looked amazing for their biological age. **What a beautiful group of women!** We also heard many heartwarming stories. One woman had just left an abusive marriage and said to us, "Even if I don't get picked, just trying out has given me so much self-confidence." Another was dealing with the challenges of MS and wanted to prove to herself that she could still do anything she really put her mind to.

Jean felt it was important when selecting our team to look at *attitude first and foremost*. Having established that criteria early on, it was easy to see which of these women could rise to the occasion with energy, focus, and dedication. Great job, Jean!

The day was spectacular! The vendors we had invited to participate brought new and innovative thinking to all who attended. From getting fitted for a bra—Let's get those boobs hoisted up so we can see them! (there was a curtain cubicle for that)—to a bodysuit that takes inches off your body and helps you lose weight, to sleepwear that absorbs the perspiration when you are having "hot flashes" (and then deodorizes it), to books and oils to use for your sex life. Questions were professionally answered about plastic surgery, and we demonstrated a flat iron that performs a multitude of tricks on your hair without scorching it beyond recognition, plus hair extensions. People could see what they looked like with long hair—it was a riot. Some looked really good (and some "not so good"; actually, downright scary!).

It was an absolute FUN, FUN day! *AND* at the end of the festivities we had eighteen beautiful Aging But DANGEROUS **models!** (The oldest turned eighty that year—bet you can't guess which one.) Hang on while we change the perception of age-appropriate fashion and who should be modeling it.

Congratulations, women!

JAZZED UP AND GORGEOUS!

THERE ARE TWO SCHOOLS of thought about visualizing something you want very badly in your life. One is that if you conjure up too grandiose a picture of what you would like, you are sure to be disappointed. We reject this. The official Aging But DANGEROUS philosophy is that if you put your most magnificent vision into the universe and it comes from a place of passion and faith, then it will happen exactly as your mind has seen it or even *better*. Opening yourself up to accept magnificence is an essential part of this entire drill. Add a little hard work to that formula, and it is failsafe.

On April 22, 2010, our most extreme vision became reality. Right before our eyes, over 500 women (and a few men) engaged in an evening of pure joy and energy—it was magical for all. From the moment the Aging But DANGEROUS Kick Ass Modeling Squad stepped onto the runway, the audience engaged and somehow became one. *Dispelling The Myths of Age and Fashion Show* touched many—some profoundly. One member of our *ABD* community said that she couldn't stop smiling when she left the event. She said, "I left the show knowing that I could still look and feel sexy, even at my age. You have given me an entirely new perspective of how I should be looking at myself."

Many who came by themselves felt the palpable camaraderie in the room and established new friendships with former strangers. Others brought old friends and commented, "We haven't had so much fun in years."

Let your hair down and feel life! That was our consistent message. One sassy seventy-plus-year-old was going to take her husband to look at the bright yellow Porsche Boxster that lurked stealthily beside the event's entrance with the subliminal message, *Buy Me*. She could barely contain her excitement. It had served its purpose. (We hope she is behind the wheel right now.)

Then, as you walked in the door to the brightly-colored, candlelit, Haitian-themed room, you immediately heard the sounds of Marion Robinson IV and his mellow, sensual, penetrating jazz renditions. Servers passing wine and hors d'oeuvres filtered throughout the venue as guests shopped at the faux Haitian village, purchasing *Vespa* motor scooters, fabulous jewelry from *FarahBean*, bags from *Drive By (Bitchin') Bags,* and unique treasures like plantable confetti from *Suka-Rama*.

Whether you were consulting with our wellness doctor, Barbro Brost, DC, from *The Brost Clinic*, participating in *Jon Charles' Blow Dry Boot Camp,* or signing up to join Aging But DANGEROUS.com, everyone seemed to be having a blast.

When Sheila Raye Charles belted out her first song to signal the start of the show, you better believe people wanted to take their seats and be thoroughly entertained. We love it when Sheila does the imitation of her sunglasses-attired dad and mimics his uniquely Ray Charles movements. It's almost scary how well she can channel his energy. She rocked the house.

Then it was time for the models, who only three short months earlier had answered a casting call that said, *"If you have always dreamed of being a model but could never find the courage... it's not too late... This is your chance."* In January, Aging But DANGEROUS put together a group of inexperienced, mostly unpolished women to represent the ABD philosophy—that it's all about attitude—*and represent us they did!*

Wow—we are still talking about how eighteen women who in most cases walked more like construction workers than models could, through their newly developed skills, bring 500 women to a near frenzy. Amazing!

Our magical evening is now a beautiful memory for all who attended. Our vision became reality because we *truly* believed it would happen—and it did. We have 500 witnesses.

DOES HE NEED A SPANXING?

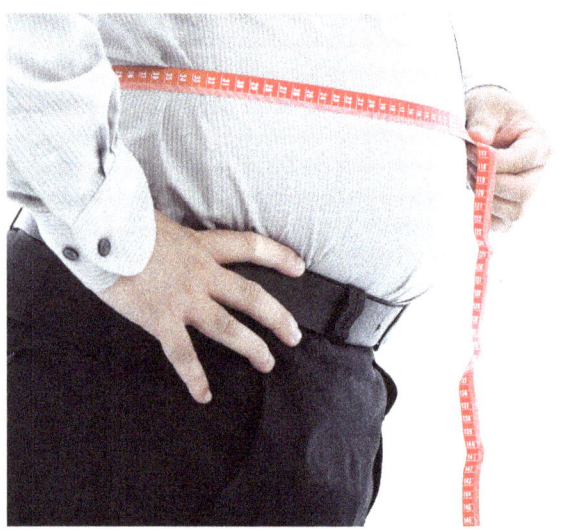

IT SEEMS LIKE every Aging But DANGEROUS woman we know is struggling with an unwanted bulge. Although there are many opportunities on the female body for this "added attraction" to occur, *my* primary focus is the tummy. There seem to be a *ton* of other women who will commiserate with my flat-to-flab frustrations. Oh, and do we see a few men on that bandwagon, also?

When Spanx introduced its men's "shapewear," the product immediately became an easy layup for late-night comedians and talk show hosts. But who is laughing now? *Neiman Marcus*, the retailer that launched this "man girdle," couldn't keep them in stock. Now there are several major retailers—*Saks, Nordstrom's, Bloomie's* the following day—hawking this new category for men, as well as several manufacturers in addition to Spanx, including Equmen and Sculptees.

Online sales of these new "enhancers" are even stronger than in the stores. Men seem to want to wear them, but they don't really want to be seen buying them. (*Chuckle, chuckle*.)

This new phenomenon looks like a regular T-shirt but has a magic internal sucking vortex at the midsection. Another product that is referred to as "profile-enhancing" underwear is like a push-up bra for men (the man bra)—sorry, but we just can't go there. The visual is way too much at this point.

Men don't seem to be calling each other to expound on how delighted they are with their new-found body enhancers, either. In fact, it seems to be very hush, hush. And should a guy's friends discover his new undergarments, a standard reply is some line about "support for his back"—yeah, yeah, yeah.

Hey, let's tell these stud muffins to relax—it's fine. No one will think less of them for caring about their shape. In fact, we think it is sexy that a guy would be confident enough to seek a little extra help for some of the frustrations that are inevitably part of this wonderful path we call aging.

So if "sucking it in" is making your guy turn a little blue from oxygen deprivation or if he never learned that concept to begin with, *Spanx him*! He just may like those compression garments a lot more that he could ever imagine. www.freshpair.com.

RUTHIE'S SHOE REJUVENATION

SEVERAL MONTHS AGO, while I was visiting my mother as she recovered from a pesky surgery, my mom expressed her desire to die—yes, die. She said she was old, tired, in pain, and that she prayed for an angel to come and help her transition to heaven.

However, later that day, she felt better and decided shoe shopping would be uplifting and medicinal. Her only caveat was that I let her go as she was. Her appearance at that point is best described as bag-ladyish. "Frightening" might also apply. In jest, I made her promise that, if we ran into any of my friends, she would duck behind a counter. She agreed; we departed.

With her cane in hand, she gradually emerged from the car and headed slowly but surely for the shoes. Our first challenge was finding sales help. She looked like a deranged escapee from the medical center. Her oversized, elastic-waist jeans would slip downward with each step until it seemed inevitable that at any moment they would drop to the floor. I pointed my phone guiltlessly to capture the hilarity, should that occur. We laughed and played until seven pairs of shoes were in her "to buy" pile. All were darling!

She seemed amazingly rejuvenated: exhausted but with a restored internal energy. Shoes will do that to a woman. My newfound role as her shoe sherpa brought a twinkle to her eye. Her depression lifted and her attitude adjusted for the positive.

The next morning, there was no talk of dying, angels, or pain. Shoe reviewal was of primary focus that day. Her delight grew with each pair she revisited. They were all perfect, as was her life—today. These days, sanity is relative, not *a* relative.

Everyone's life is measured in feet, one step at a time, as how we "walk our talk." Even at ninety years old, doing it in stylish shoes, or shoes you feel you look good in, adds an extra boost to life. I've heard if the shoe fits, wear it. And as for my mom, she will.

> ## A Brief Diversion
>
>   An Aging But DANGEROUS-kind of woman is never too old to live her dreams. Be bold, be inspired and enjoy pushing the preconceived notion of what might be appropriate for you. Try this link on and see if it fits.
>
> http://www.cbsnews.com/video/watch/?id=7390506n&tag=contentMain;contentBody

BLINDED
by the light...

"...revved up like a deuce,
Another runner in the night..."

(Finally you know what Manfred Mann's Earth Band was really saying!)

A FRENCH CONNECTION

WHEN CINDY WALKS into the room with her darling face, her beautiful spirit, and her sparkling eyes, the *last* thing that comes to your mind is "stroke victim." But that is exactly what she is.

Adventure took on a whole new meaning in 2002 when, at the age of fifty-one, Cindy had a major stroke that left her unable to speak and the right side of her body paralyzed.

On the Monday a week prior to her stroke, she had a migraine and collapsed. That afternoon, when she attempted to remove her contact lenses, she put her finger in her nose; her hands, eyes, and brain had stopped working together. After a trip to the emergency room, a little morphine, and a few tests, the hospital sent her home.

On that Friday, her migraine repeated itself (only now the symptoms were back and more of a concern). A trip back to the emergency room led to more morphine and another dismissal.

One week into this nightmare, on Memorial Day, Cindy awoke from a nap with almost no coordination between what she was thinking that she wanted to do and what she was able to do. She headed for a different hospital this time. She was admitted and tests began—but she didn't really understand anything they were asking her to do. "I was there, but I wasn't there."

When she awoke the following morning, she had lapsed into a full-blown stroke: no speech, no mobility in her right side. She had no idea what was going on. Later that morning, in the cath lab, she watched the inside of her own brain as doctors prepared to remove the clot she had developed. She felt like an observer in some strange time warp as they began doing the reconnaissance work for stents and basic artery repair.

Cindy said, "I felt like I was on vacation, I felt a sense of euphoria. I thought I would be fine in a couple of weeks."

About a week or so after the surgery, she asked her kids what had happened. Her predicament was just beginning to sink in. When she heard a recounting of the events that had led to that moment, she was devastated. It was the first time that she had really understood this catastrophic situation.

Occupational, physical, and speech therapy began immediately, and it was exhausting. She had to re-learn *everything*.

But then the *huge* anomaly of this tragic event became apparent: when she regained her ability to speak, she had a heavy French accent. Her speech therapist tried to get rid of it but to no avail. Cindy says she really doesn't mind, but that it slows her down. Her response to enquiries about her accent depends upon the circumstances and her frame of mind. "People don't believe me anyway, even when I tell them the truth," she says, sounding very French. It is when people start speaking French to her that the adorable French accent becomes problematic.

Cindy wants to share her optimism through public speaking. "Never, *ever* let go of your will to do better and don't give up hope," is her message. "People need support and encouragement with their individual recovery. I would like to help give that to them." To that *we* say *tres bien*!

To read more about this unusual yet quite real phenomenon, follow this link. https://en.wikipedia.org/wiki/Foreign_accent_syndrome.

A Brief Diversion

- Don't get too crotchety and cheap to sport the lace undies like the French—your hoo-ha is worth it.
- "I would love to speak a foreign language, but I can't. So I grew hair under my arms instead"—Sue Kolensky

IN YOUR ZONE

BLUE ZONES HAVE become a hot topic of late. Prior to this recent buzz about idyllic living, I thought blue zones were what happened when we forgot to take our hormones—not so. Blue Zones are places where people live longer, healthier lives. First popularized by an article in *National Geographic* in the 1970s, these areas have no geographic commonality. They are scattered all over the world—go figure.

So why would we go to Abkhazia (a region in the Republic of Georgia), when we can create our own "blue" zone slightly closer to home? Let's call it the Aging But DANGEROUS *Slightly Fuchsia Pink Zone.*

With Oprah "retired," juicing gone bananas, and articles ad nauseam about the topic of living healthier, happier lives, the tools are readily available for us to build this wonderful *personal* zone where we can be healthy, happy, and long-lived. And our zone is portable.

Here is the outrageously simple formula that you and I could follow for this *huge* payoff. Puzzling to me is why don't we?

Eat Organic: Pay more, eat less. Like I had to go to Vilcambamba, Ecuador (a not-so-conveniently located "blue zone") to figure that out. But there, it's pay less, eat more, and still look great in the tourist garb.

Eat fruits and vegetables: A hex on processed foods. Yes, Mom, I know you have been telling me that my entire life.

Stay active: Always. So when Jean and her husband (the 70s crowd) do Body Attack (Cardio Kick Boxing), I should try to be supportive instead of falling into hysterics just imagining what that must look like.

Have a positive attitude about aging: That IS Aging But DANGEROUS.

Eat healthy fats: Like no Krispy Kreme donuts (Okay, maybe once in a blue moon you could leave your blue zone).

Laugh and share your joy: Wallow in joy with the people that you care about.

We don't have to go to the Hunza Valley in Pakistan to find a Blue Zone—*create your own*. We only need to get off our proverbial tushies and put a little effort into the best life ever. Like my friend's Aunt Gretle use to say, "You rest, you rust."

I'm going to the Aging But DANGEROUS Slightly Fuchsia Pink Zone. Reduce your "but," join me, and we'll live happily ever after, totally zoned.

I'VE SEEN THE LIGHT

FOR YEARS I STRUGGLED with a weird, weighty feeling that came over me in the fall. Part of me loved the crisp days, beautiful autumn colors, and romantic delusions of snuggling up with Mr. Wonderful on a chilly fall evening. But part of me turned into robo-bitch: the sometimes grumpy, sometimes short-tempered, most of the time drag-ass person who haunted my every October.

It wasn't always this way; my symptoms seem to increase with the number of candles fueling the small inferno on my birthday cake. (Even though some studies report that this experience lessens with senior status, I have not experienced that.)

Lucky for me, my therapist diagnosed Seasonal Affective Disorder (SAD) and suggested I start sitting under a light specifically designed to treat this condition. Bingo! Weight lifted, grumpiness dissipated, short temper elongated. Ass still drags periodically—that's usually sleep-related.

It took me several years to commit to light therapy (to see the light, so to speak), even after I was diagnosed. I was sure I could resolve this issue solo. I was wrong! There are many options for lights on line, but I happen to be thrilled with my "BOX-elite" from http://www.northernlighttechnologies.com. These are the gold standard, according to the Mayo Clinic.

In order to be affective, the light must be 10,000 lux (lux is a measurement of light intensity), and you must sit 12-18 inches from the light with open eyes for thirty minutes. You do *not* need to look directly into the light; you can read, knit, etc.

Since I started therapeutically illuminating myself, I have shared my story with others who have been thrilled to know that they are not the only people annoyed (sometimes almost incapacitated) by these sobering symptoms. The American Academy of Family Physicians states that "as many as six of every 100 people in the United States have SAD. Another 10% to 20% may experience some mild form of SAD. It seems to be more common in women than men, and although some children and teenagers get SAD, it usually doesn't start in people younger than twenty years of age. SAD is more common in northern geographic regions."

Symptoms of Seasonal Affective Disorder include:

- Depressed mood
- Irritability
- Hopelessness
- Anxiety
- Loss of energy
- Social withdrawal
- Oversleeping (feeling like you want to hibernate)
- Appetite changes, especially a craving for sweet or starchy foods
- Weight gain
- Difficulty concentrating and processing information
- A heavy feeling in the arms or legs
- A drop in energy level
- Fatigue

The intensity of my therapy light connotes *Back to The Future* flashbacks. I am sure that this odd glow coming from my bedroom window has perplexed my neighbors and titillated their overly-active imaginations. If they only knew that without my light my head would spin on a 360-degree rotation and fire would come off the end of my tongue. No surprise that Mr. Wonderful is only a figment of my imagination.

For the light at the end of your tunnel, try the following:

http://www.northernlighttechnologies.com/
http://www.psychtreatment.com/seasonal_affective_disorder.htm

TELL ME, WHAT IS IT YOU PLAN TO DO

WITH YOUR ONE WILD & PRECIOUS LIFE?

••• Mary Oliver

DECIDE TO LIVE

AGING BUT DANGEROUS continues to forge a path through the jungle of preconceived notions and cockamamie ideas that most of us have conjured up, or been brainwashed with, about our aging selves. More and more people are discovering a simple truth: risk, aka "danger", as many would see it, is an aphrodisiac for life. Someone said, "if you're not living on the edge, you're taking up too much space." Bravo!

One person's risk is another person's boredom, so no one can tell you what risk means to you—but you. Once on the CBS *Sunday Morning Show,* Ben Stein shared his curmudgeonly wisdom in a style only he can conjure up.

He said that he asked his shrink, a super-smart guy, how he would generally divide up the people who were happy in life from those who were not.

Mr. Stein said he answered like a shot.

He told Mr. Stein that the unhappy ones are people who let their parents or their family talk them into doing something for a career that didn't really fit them. These people wanted to be writers or performers, but instead decided to take the cautious route to accountancy school or law school or dental school.

The happy ones he told Mr Stein were the ones who made a decision to live. They decided to do what their hearts told them to do, what was in them to do. They took risks and they took chances, trying a lot of different things until they got to where they wanted to be.

Most of them worked incredibly hard and sometimes lived on the edge. But it got them to where they could look back on their life and feel it wasn't wasted.

Mr. Stein felt his advice was spectacular!

You have to earn your keep, even if you are born rich. But to decide to live – that makes a lot of difference in this difficult world.

Mr. Stein challenged us to choose to live a life you want to live, not one that's safe or what someone else thinks you should do.

Decide to live.

Wisdom like that referenced above are part of the giant mental machete that Aging But DANGEROUS is wielding to penetrate the thick jungle of habit that holds many of us captive in a myriad of excuses as to why we "can't." WE CAN! It is not too late for most of us to do what is truly in us.

After Jean's brief interview on Channel 11's *"The Weekend Show"*, (the NBC affiliate in Minneapolis), concerning our now annual Martini Jump Skydive in August of 2010, we had almost 100 women email us wanting to jump. We set a world record that year with 107 women over the age of 50, skydiving in one day. Most of them said that skydiving was something they had always wanted to do. You might say that they had *decided to live!*

A Brief Diversion

- When the weather cooperates with great energy and purpose, you can conjure up a perfect day. Yesterday, at the 2010 Aging But DANGEROUS Martini Jump Skydive all these wonderful elements converged to create a day, that those attending, will not soon forget.

- Motives for even wanting to bail out of a moving airplane varied for our jumpers: from just conquering cancer, to just being diagnosed with cancer, from recent divorce, to recently starting over in a new relationship, from having unexpectedly being laid off from long time employment, to having just acquired the job of a life time, from just having suffered a great loss: a mother or a husband or a son, to overcoming a variety of phobias. Skydiving seems to be a rite of passage to overcome fears, celebrate victories and commemorate occasions. Aging But DANGEROUS does it because it's such fun!!

REACH!

...the tragedy in life does not lie in not reaching your goal. The tragedy lies in having no goal to reach. It isn't a calamity to die with dreams unfulfilled, but it is a calamity not to dream. It is not a disaster to be unable to capture you ideal, but it is a disaster to have no ideal to capture. It is not a disgrace not to reach the stars, but it is a disgrace to have no stars to reach for.

···Benjamin E. Mays

RESOURCES

Additional information on Urination Incontinence:
- Visit http://kidney.niddk.nih.gov/kudiseases/pubs/uiwomen/
- Google "urinary incontinence" and make sure you are on a reputable site like Mayo Clinic, the University of CA San Francisco, the Urology Care Foundation, or the National Institutes of Health site mentioned above
- To learn more go to the Mayo Clinic and search *urinary incontinence in women*: http://www.mayoclinic.org/diseases-conditions/urinary-incontinence/basics/causes/con-20037883
- http://www.ucsf.edu/news/2015/07/130996/postmenopausal-women-depression-or-urinary-incontinence-experience-vaginal
- http://www.urologyhealth.org/urologic-conditions/urinary-incontinence
- "The Truth Behind Six Incontinence Myths": http://www.everydayhealth.com/incontinence/the-truth-behind-six-incontinence-myths.aspx

Downsizing and Purging:
Find some great resources are available at:
- http://ohioline.osu.edu/ss-fact/0214.html
- https://www.pinterest.com/explore/downsizing-tips/

Apartment design and space-saving resources:
- http://www.apartmenttherapy.com/-good-questions-16-29316
- https://www.google.com/#q=charles+rennie+mackintosh+furniture
- http://www.yliving.com/category/Bath-Towels/Beach-Towels/_/N-3ku3kZ3ku34
- There are many many Feng Shui websites, like:
- http://fengshui.about.com/od/fengshuicures/qt/fengshuicolor.htm

The *Better Homes and Garden* Color-a-Room website:
http://www.bhg.com/decorating/color/colors/welcome-to-color-a-room

Urban Farming:
If you visit www.urbanchicken.org, you will be amazed at the information and options offered to the urban chicken owner.

Reduce your Carbon Footprint:
Visit www.replayground.com for some great info, as well as some highly tricked-out project suggestions.

Rejuvenation ideas:
- Goat's milk ice cream at www.laloos.com: it's udderly delicious!
- How about M&Ms? www.mms.com
- the new, glamorous, glitter-infused, scented, multi-shaded, glow-in-the-dark Crayon. www.crayola.com

Creative Visualization:

Visit www.shaktigawain.com to learn more about creative visualization.

Woolly Wally Vertical Gardens and Organic garden information:

- For information on installation, picking the right soil, choosing the perfect plants or just tracking Wally down, go to www.woollypocket.com/qa.php.
- For more information, go to: www.uos.harvard.edu/fmo/landscape/organiclandscaping. The grass truly is greener on their side of the fence.

For feeling sexy! Refer to the following links for more hot information:

- http://bestofeverythingafter50.com/tag/feeling-invisible-after-50/
- http://www.babyboomers-lifes-pleasures.com/feel-sexier.html

Great Posture Inspiration:

All the following links will inspire you to suck that gut in and stick that chest out no matter how tired you feel.

- http://www.bhg.com/health-family/fitness/workouts-programs/exercises-to-improve-your-posture/
- http://www.oprah.com/health/Back-Posture-Help-Exercises-to-Stand-Up-Straight
- http://www.naturalnews.com/030956_posture_health.html
- http://www.kellogg.northwestern.edu/News_Articles/2011/powerful-posture.aspx

Information on the 20# Club:
To be fed guidance, information and cheerleading, go to: www.agingbutdangerous.com and click on 20# Club.

Not a Perfect Pair?
http://www.pickyourperfectpairbras.com/

For Spanx:
www.freshpair.com.

Information on strokes and Foreign-language Syndrome:
To read more about this unusual yet quite real phenomenon, follow this link. https://en.wikipedia.org/wiki/Foreign_accent_syndrome.

Information on SAD/Light at the end of the tunnel:
- http://www.northernlighttechnologies.com/
- http://www.psychtreatment.com/seasonal_affective_disorder.htm

PHOTO CREDITS

1. **pg. 7**—My Mom – Ruthie A. Bates, personal collection

2. **pg. 15**—PARTNER IN CRIME (4 photos) Aging But DANGEROUS.com archives.

3. **pg. 20**—Restroom sign by Apples Eyes Studio, http://www.shutterstock.com/pic.mhtml?id=189021968&src=id, licensed under Shutterstock Standard Agreement.

   Man covering his crotch by Kaspars Grinvalds, http://www.shutterstock.com/pic.mhtml?id=257216062&src=id, licensed under Shutterstock Standard Agreement.

   Red dressed woman by Iakov Filimonov, http://www.shutterstock.com/pic.mhtml?id=272112233&src=id, licensed under Shutterstock Standard Agreement.

4. **pg. 23**—Woman squatting by George Allen Penton, http://www.shutterstock.com/pic.mhtml?id=151720913&src=id, licensed under Shutterstock Standard Agreement.

5. **pg. 28**—Woman in box by otnaydur, http://www.shutterstock.com/pic.mhtml?id=31886887&src=id, licensed under Shutterstock Standard Agreement.

   Stack of chairs by mariakraynova, http://www.shutterstock.com/pic.mhtml?id=209842555&src=id, licensed under Shutterstock Standard Agreement.

6. pg. 37—Interior photo by Marty Lang, Lava Submarine Studio

7. pg. 40—Interior photo Marty Lang, Lava Submarine Studio

8. pg. 45—Interior photo Marty Lang, Lava Submarine Studio

9. pg. 48—Yellow wall with blue chair by Joy Brown, http://www.shutterstock.com/pic.mhtml?id=17970703&src=id, licensed under Shutterstock Standard Agreement.

10. pg. 52—Envelopes and heart by Africa Studio, http://www.shutterstock.com/pic.mhtml?id=250217707&src=id, licensed under Shutterstock Standard Agreement.

11. pg. 55—Red chicken by Vadym Zaitsev, http://www.shutterstock.com/pic.mhtml?id=129765431&src=id, licensed under Shutterstock Standard Agreement.

    Black chicken by Jacqueline Abromeit, http://www.shutterstock.com/pic.mhtml?id=56501767&src=id, licensed under Shutterstock Standard Agreement.

    White chicken by WilleeCole Photography, http://www.shutterstock.com/pic.mhtml?id=174049772&src=id, licensed under Shutterstock Standard Agreement.

12. pg. 58—MOVIN' ON (4 photos) Aging But DANGEROUS.com archives.

13. pg. 60—Woman in shell/Wikipedia

14. pg. 63—Collage with world by T.L. Furrer, http://www.shutterstock.com/pic.mhtml?id=190009082&src=id, licensed under Shutterstock Standard Agreement.

15. pg. 68—Footprint by Lana Veshta, http://www.shutterstock.com/pic.mhtml?id=296607521&src=id, licensed under Shutterstock Standard Agreement.

16. pg. 73—Woman flashing by Marty Lang, Lava Submarine Studio

17. pg. 75—Cat by Susan Schmitz, http://www.shutterstock.com/pic.mhtml?id=307038581&src=id, licensed under Shutterstock Standard Agreement.

18. pg. 76—Chili pepper, http://www.shutterstock.com/pic.mhtml?id=303580547&src=id, licensed under Shutterstock Standard Agreement.

19. pg. 80—Nude from back by Anetta, http://www.shutterstock.com/pic.mhtml?id=296620712&src=id, licensed under Shutterstock Standard Agreement.

20. pg. 83—Women on beach by Bench Woman, FreakingNews.com

21. pg. 86—Haircut/Hair Raising by Julenochek, http://www.shutterstock.com/pic.mhtml?id=303043388&src=id, licensed under Shutterstock Standard Agreement.

22. pg. 88—Naked ping pong by Jack Taylor photographer, Bancroft Media.

23. pg. 90—Triangular sign with people by Becky Stares, http://www.shutterstock.com/pic.mhtml?id=47370691&src=id, licensed under Shutterstock Standard Agreement.

24. pg. 92—Eye by LuckyImages, http://www.shutterstock.com/pic.mhtml?id=27624565&src=id, licensed under Shutterstock Standard Agreement.

25. pg. 93—Multiple eyebrows by Uliana Gureeva, http://www.shutterstock.com/pic.mhtml?id=109851722&src=id, licensed under Shutterstock Standard Agreement.

26. pg. 95—Feet with flower by Micolas, http://www.shutterstock.com/pic.mhtml?id=280750829&src=id, licensed under Shutterstock Standard Agreement.

27. pg. 97—Measuring tape on fork by johnfoto18, http://www.shutterstock.com/pic.mhtml?id=266405411&src=id, licensed under Shutterstock Standard Agreement.

28. pg. 102—Yellow crane by Levente Naghi, http://www.shutterstock.com/pic.mhtml?id=232177402&src=id, licensed under Shutterstock Standard Agreement.

29. pg. 104—Two cups by irakite, http://www.shutterstock.com/pic.mhtml?id=73772209&src=id, licensed under Shutterstock Standard Agreement.

30. pg. 106—T-shirt by Di Studio, http://www.shutterstock.com/pic.mhtml?id=270981815&src=id, licensed under Shutterstock Standard Agreement.

31. pg. 112—Man in kilt by Elnur, http://www.shutterstock.com/pic.mhtml?id=313461101&src=id, licensed under Shutterstock Standard Agreement.

32. pg. 114—Skirts by Mr.Exen, http://www.shutterstock.com/pic.mhtml?id=229254055&src=id, licensed under Shutterstock Standard Agreement.

33. pg. 116—JEAN'S JEANS (3 photos) Aging But DANGEROUS.com archives.

34. pg. 119—Surprised woman by Serhiy Kobyakov, http://www.shutterstock.com/pic.mhtml?id=113527912&src=id, licensed under Shutterstock Standard Agreement.

35. pg. 124 & 127—Women modeling (5 photos) Aging But DANGEROUS.com archives.

36. pg. 128—Man's tummy by Tom Wang, http://www.shutterstock.com/pic.mhtml?id=197093498&src=id, licensed under Shutterstock Standard Agreement.

37. pg. 136—French item collage by totallyPic.com, http://www.shutterstock.com/pic.mhtml?id=283395428&src=id, licensed under Shutterstock Standard Agreement.

38. pg. 140—Warrior pose figure by InesBazdar, http://www.shutterstock.com/pic.mhtml?id=245011159&src=id, licensed under Shutterstock Standard Agreement.

39. pg. 143—Face with lights by Agsandrew, http://www.shutterstock.com/pic.mhtml?id=164294282&src=id, licensed under Shutterstock Standard Agreement.

40. pg. 147—Woman with light bulb over head by Ollyy, http://www.shutterstock.com/pic.mhtml?id=176264936&src=id, licensed under Shutterstock Standard Agreement.

41. pg. 148—Women at ABD skydiving event (5 photos) Aging But DANGEROUS.com archives.

42. pg. 151—Reaching for star, Marty Lang, Lava Submarine Studio

THANKS, MOM...!

MY ENTIRE LIFE there has been one person who has consistently believed in me, encouraged me, supported me and defended me, **my Mom!**

Thank you, Mom. You are my rock, my inspiration, and the source of much of my off-the-wall humor. I love you!

There is another person without whom Jean and I could not have accomplished many of our goals, like sanity, and probably this book. Thank you, Pat Maltz, for your amazing capacity to fill in our blanks and for endlessly backstopping us in all of our endeavors.

To be blessed by the multitudes of spectacular women in my life is overwhelming at times. To all of you who aided in this undertaking, I am forever grateful and love you all very deeply!

Thank you, thank you, one and all!

Most importantly, thank you God for putting all these bizarre thoughts in my head and giving me the fortitude to withstand this grueling process. We did it!

ABOUT THE AUTHOR

SUZANNE RECEIVED HER Bachelor of Fine Arts degree from Stephens College and is a recipient of its Excellence in Art Award. She completed extended studies in Europe and a graduate-level certificate program at Harvard University's, Graduate School of Design. She was the first nationally certified interior designer in Minnesota and is a longtime member of IIDA. She also briefly attended her family-owned business school because her father told her that if she could type she would never starve. Her highest marks were in penmanship.

Suzanne founded the award-winning Design Syndicate, Inc. (DSI) and was a vital force in the Minneapolis design community for over three decades. Her firm received a national reputation for innovative, functional and cost-effective work and boasted an extensive list of internationally renowned clientele including Yoplait, ConAgra, John Deere, Mayo Clinic, 3M, and the singer formerly known as Prince.

Suzanne served as design editor for *Twin Cities Magazine*. She has spoken extensively about interior design and also developed and presented a weekly segment for the Minneapolis NBC affiliates television show *Corporate Video*. She topped off her design career as regional marketing director for HOK Architects, at that time the world's largest architectural firm.

Since co-founding Aging But DANGEROUS in 2008, she rarely sleeps, she drinks heavily, and she dreams of living in a monastery where no one can find her. In addition to their weekly radio show, *Aging But DANGEROUS SIZZLE*, monthly events, saving women over fifty from the tragedy of being ignored by society, fielding interviews by *Time* magazine, and fighting off the ever-more-aggressive paparazzi, she and Jean consume serious quantities of tranquillizers and pray for world peace.

Filling Suzanne's personal life are four adult children (one is a cancer survivor), six grandchildren, a variety of exercise regimens, her own personal growth and continually deepening her spirituality. Her passions include contemporary art, boating, gardening, and Team Ghana (an organization she co-founded in the late '90s to empower the women and children of rural Ghana). Suzanne is also an accomplished equestrian with multiple national championships to her credit.

In 2001, she and her former spouse co-chaired World Presidents Organization (WPO) Education Committee for the Twin Cities chapter, winning a First Place Award for "Best Program of the Year" (Internationally).

A glimpse inside her psyche would reveal an intensely energetic and spontaneous woman with a thirst for knowledge that is partially driven by her lifelong struggle with A.D.H.D. and minor learning disabilities. Her commitment to empowering women was instilled in her by her mother and grandmother, who were clearly capable of being so much more than society encouraged them to be. Her humor and appreciation of the smallest details remain her fuel for life.

www.ingramcontent.com/pod-product-compliance
Lightning Source LLC
Chambersburg PA
CBHW040328300426
44113CB00020B/2688